What People Are Saying about Be Last

My good friend Jeremy has done it once again. He has encouraged us to not only *know* that there is abundant life beyond ourselves, but to know *how* to find and achieve that abundant life. We discover it by following Jesus' example of dying to ourselves and putting others before us. Jeremy kindly reminds us all of this great message. **—MAC POWELL, LEAD SINGER, THIRD DAY**

Every generation needs the truth of God's Word presented and applied in fresh, new ways. Jeremy Kingsley is just the dynamic voice to do that for today, and his heart and passion are on vivid display in *Be Last*. You'll love Jeremy's unique personal style, but what's more important, you will be powerfully challenged and inspired to come alive and live the life, the abundant life Jesus came to give. **—WES STAFFORD, PRESIDENT AND CEO, COMPASSION INTERNATIONAL**

Being last, or at least being willing to be last, is the way you struggle upward toward first place in God's view of success. There is no humility without humiliation, said Bernard Clairvaux. Still, God doesn't want anyone to end up last. It's just that last is the springboard by which we dive upward into heaven's esteem. Jeremy Kingsley has made it clear that, spiritually speaking, gravity is a lie. Gethsemane, it is true, put a lot of downward stress on the majesty of Christ. But isn't it amazing, the grave was completely without gravity on Easter morning! And when the last rocks have trembled and Christ stands belted at the chest with golden splendor, Kingsley will have proved to all of us that we serve a Savior who wasn't afraid to wade through humiliation on the way to exaltation. **—CALVIN MILLER,** SPEAKER, PAINTER, AND AUTHOR OF MORE THAN FORTY BOOKS OF THEOLOGY AND INSPIRATION

A lover of God and a student of God's Word, Jeremy Kingsley is passionate about serving Jesus and others with life-altering truth! The application of these pages could alter an entire generation. I've been an eyewitness of Jeremy's commitment to the message of this book while he powerfully served as a lead itinerant speaker with Kingdom Building Ministries. With inspiring energy and experience, Jeremy writes from the depths of his own heart and journey! **—DWIGHT ROBERTSON,** PRESIDENT AND FOUNDER, KINGDOM BUILDING MINISTRIES

In *Be Last: Descending to Greatness,* Jeremy Kingsley drives home one of my deepest principles of life and leadership: *It's not about you.* Jeremy's love of Jesus and the Bible shines through in every chapter, and his message speaks directly to the reader as if it were a personal conversation. Live your life with a servant's heart. Read this book. **—KEN BLANCHARD,** COAUTHOR OF *THE ONE MINUTE MANAGER* AND *LEAD LIKE JESUS*

Be Last is a testament to the tremendous work of humility God has done in the heart of Jeremy Kingsley. Jeremy's contagious passion for true servanthood is palpable on every page and will inspire readers to go against the flow of a self-centered and misguided culture to find greatness the only way it can truly be found—by serving. **—GARY CHAPMAN,** AUTHOR OF THE BEST-SELLING BOOK *THE FIVE LOVE LANGUAGES*

Descending to Greatness

be last

JEREMY KINGSLEY

TYNDALE HOUSE PUBLISHERS, INC.
Carol Stream, Illinois

Library of Congress Cataloging-in-Publication Data

Kingsley, Jeremy.
    Be last : descending to greatness / Jeremy Kingsley.
      p. cm.
    ISBN-13: 978-1-4143-1641-3 (sc)
    ISBN-10: 1-4143-1641-0 (sc)
1. Christian life.   I. Title.
BV4501.3.K5575 2008
248.4—dc22   2008005573

Printed in the United States of America

14   13   12   11   10   09   08

7   6   5   4   3   2   1

To my immediate family: my wife, Dawn, and my sons,
Jaden and Dylan.

✦

To my birth family: parents, Randy and Virjean,
and brothers, Jeff and J. R.

✦

To my church family at Gateway.

✦

To the Onelife Ministries family: the board of directors, advisory team,
prayer partners, and financial givers.

✦

To the family of believers worldwide who are truly pursuing
greatness through humility and service.

✦

And finally, to Jesus. I hope this makes you smile.

Contents

Preface

It all started with a T-shirt.

Some time ago I was speaking at a music festival in Pennsylvania when a representative from Tyndale House Publishers came to hear me speak and afterward to talk about a manuscript I had written called *One Step Closer*. As we walked the grounds, we came to my resource table, where people could purchase CDs, books, and T-shirts.

"What's that?" my Tyndale friend asked, pointing to a shirt with the simple words **Be Last** printed boldly on the front.

I told him that being last was one of the key messages I speak on.

"What exactly do you mean by that?"

I've actually had that question asked of me many times, and it has always provided a great opportunity to share a truth that I believe is greatly lacking in the Christian community. "Well," I said, "it's about humility and service and trying to always put Jesus and other people first. Jesus said that's how we become great—by being last."

"Okay," he said, to my surprise. "Let's put *One Step Closer* on hold for now. I want you write a book on that!"

So here it is.

Acknowledgments

I would like to express my deepest gratitude to the faculty and staff of Columbia International University for their investment in teaching me how "To Know Him and Make Him Known."

I would also like to thank Kingdom Building Ministries for years of continued support and encouragement to my family and ministry.

Last, but certainly not least, thanks to Paul T. Penley and Creston Mapes for their help in transcribing messages, editing, and sharing their insights on portions of this book.

Introduction: Graduating to Greatness

Remember when you graduated from high school or college? Maybe there was talk of parties with friends, neighbors, and relatives. Your dad may have pulled out that old tie that made you feel sweaty and ridiculous, and your mom was on an emotional roller coaster because her little baby was all grown up and moving on.

If you were anything like me, you almost missed graduation altogether! In high school, I not only wore the hat of class clown but also lacked motivation, as evidenced by grades of "Incomplete" in simple classes such as typing (yes, that was "B.C."—before computers). While the rest of the senior class got out of school a week early to frolic in the sun and try out their new freedom, I was forced to spend the week making up the piles of work I'd conveniently put off by acting like a moron.

That's not all. Once I *did* get on track, I still almost missed graduation. Sweating it out on the street basketball courts of Washington, D.C., in a series of intense afternoon games, I completely forgot about my high school graduation ceremony.

"Where have you been?" my mom screamed when she heard the screen door slam. "It's time to leave right now!"

Skipping the shower and grabbing my best "waiter looking" outfit—including the tie Dad had dug up—I was out the door, smelling like anything but a graduation rose.

What was your graduation ceremony like? How did you feel that day? Did some students get special recognition for certain accomplishments? I think, for the most part, graduation ceremonies are pretty similar. But there's one ceremony I've heard about that continues to blow me away, and even helped plant a seed in my mind for the book you hold in your hands.

That ceremony takes place each year at a Christian college that cares a great deal about academics, athletics, relationships, and most important, the spiritual development of each student. Therefore, it's only fitting that when its graduates walk across the stage, they not only shake hands with the president and receive their diplomas but also receive something much more important, much more symbolic: a towel.

Why a towel? Because as in the Bible, one of that college's core values is humility. Putting others first. Helping people. Serving. Becoming last so that Jesus can be magnified. The towel is a reminder of one of the last and most critical things Jesus did among his followers—he knelt and washed their feet. And he told his disciples to do the same.

Jesus said that he didn't come to be served but to serve (see Mark 10:45). He was spent for us, and the towel is a vivid reminder that life is not about us or about our becoming the greatest in the world's eyes by achieving some lofty personal, academic, athletic, corporate, or financial goal. Life is about serving others. It's about connecting with God and doing what he says. Jesus taught that the way up is down. The last shall be first.

So what do you say we go on a journey together? A journey to the back of the line. A journey to be last.

—*Jeremy Kingsley*

How Do I Become Great?

"Being Last" by Living a Life of Service

What tops your list of things that you're good at? Is it writing or cooking or dancing or accounting or music? Are you an accomplished engineer or the chairman of a board or a decorated athlete? Maybe you're the guy who can fix any computer problem or the woman who can parallel park on any street in the city. The options for showing off what you do well are nearly endless.

But being good at something and being great at it are not the same. There is a difference between having *strong* skills and being *great* with those skills. The same is true for our Christian experience. Maybe you're known as "pretty good," a Christian who can teach well or sing well or lead well or memorize well or serve well. Have you ever wanted your Christian experience to become great? Maybe you're not even very good at following Jesus right now but you still want to become great. That kind of hunger usually resides in those who have met Jesus and have seen how amazing he is.

When you think about your Christian experience, would you call it "great"? Would you say that you have achieved "greatness" or at least are headed in that direction? The question may be a bit too hard to ponder, but the quest for greatness is a topic worth pursuing. Of course, there is no way to determine the "greatness" of one's life with Christ until we define the word itself. And that can be a difficult task because our presumed definitions are often skewed by the surrounding culture's values.

When it comes to business, music, or sports, greatness is easier to define. For example, the statement that Michael Jordan was a great basketball player is hardly contestable. His six championships, Olympic gold medal, MVP awards, appearances on All-Star teams, scoring records, and game-winning shots prove it. His actions and awards place him above all his competitors. Boxer Muhammad Ali, football receiver Jerry Rice, and golfer Tiger Woods have accomplished similar feats in their own sports, feats that demonstrate greatness. But how do we define greatness in the Christian life? Can checking stat sheets and lists of awards provide a clear standard for evaluating the greatness of a Christian? *How do I become great?*

Is it worth expending the energy required to experience God's great life for us? Well, if *I'm* defining greatness, I don't know whether it's worth pursuing. And if *you're* defining greatness, I'm not sure you'll want to chase an arbitrary idea that you made up for yourself. But if the greatest One of all defines greatness for us, we would be wise to learn what he says—and the greatest One who has ever lived *has* spoken about greatness. The King of kings and Lord of lords has told us how we should approach the journey toward greatness. So just like golfers who pay thousands of dollars for instruction from Tiger or computer software engineers who listen intently to Michael Dell, we should drop everything and tune into Jesus' approach to greatness.

God's Cheering Section

In John 12:41 the writer explains that the prophet Isaiah saw and described the glory of Jesus in Isaiah 6. So if we want to get a taste of how great Jesus was before he came to earth as a human being, we should check out what Isaiah saw in his vision of the Messiah's glory hundreds of years before Christ came. It may take a little time for us twenty-first-century Americans to understand how profoundly Isaiah's vision depicts Jesus' greatness, but stick with me, and I'll try to explain. First, let's see what Isaiah 6:1-4 says:

> It was in the year King Uzziah died that I saw the Lord. He was sitting on a lofty throne, and the train of his robe filled the Temple. Attending him were mighty seraphim, each having six wings. With two wings they covered their faces, with two they covered their feet, and with two they flew. They were calling out to each other, "Holy, holy, holy is the LORD of Heaven's Armies! The whole earth is filled with his glory!" Their voices shook the Temple to its foundations, and the entire building was filled with smoke.

Words certainly do not do justice to what this experience would have been like for Isaiah. One moment he is praying, and the next moment he is swept into a vision of the Lord himself. He sees the inside of God's heavenly home—a temple different from the one Solomon built on Mount Zion because of the giant throne in it—and he encounters a sanctuary full of creatures bringing down the house with their alternating chants focused on Jesus.

In this vision Isaiah sees a room filled with seraphim. Now these are not the type of angels who look human or your classic

3

"two wingers." These are special beings that have three pairs of wings. Each pair of wings has a specific purpose. When these beings are in the presence of Jesus, they use one pair of wings to cover their faces out of humility. With the second pair they cover their feet out of respect. They use the third pair to maintain flight. Apparently it takes specially designed body parts to give Jesus the honor he deserves when you're in a room filled with his magnificence.

The job of the seraphim is simpler to describe than their unique physique. The seraphim have only one reason to exist: to tell God all the time how awesome he is. All they do is shout back and forth, "Holy! Holy! Holy!" and let their chants about his global glory blow up the decibel meter. They were created to be his constant cheering section, like a "divine dawg pound"! What a life! Imagine constantly getting to cheer for your favorite sports team in its home stadium and knowing that your team is the eternally undisputed world champion.

Do you understand what all this hoopla means? These heavenly beings have been created for the single purpose of chanting and cheering about Jesus' glory. That's all they do. Think about it. You've got to be indescribably great if angels have been created just to shout about you forever. Suppose you went up to one of these angels and asked, "Excuse me, Angel 3058, what is it that you do?"

Angel 3058 would reply, "I spend my time crying out how amazing Jesus is."

If you asked him, "What do you do after work?" he'd say, "There is no 'after.' I just keep calling out how great Jesus is."

If you begged him to come help you with something, he'd have to respond, "I can't stop telling Jesus how amazing he is.

We're about to start the MVP chant, and there's just no way we can have one less voice publicizing God's fame. I've got to go!"

That gives Jesus the right to define greatness for us if he desires.

When Does Jesus Teach Us How to Become Great?

If Jesus is so great, then he knows that we need him to show *us* how to become great. A few times in his life would have seemed prime opportunities for him to do that. Maybe his birth would have been a great time? If he was going to teach us how to be great, he should probably have started off his time on earth with a grand entrance. Christmas morning should have been more like the Fourth of July, with fireworks coming out of heaven to light up the whole earth. Jesus should have flown in like a comet whose blazing light dwarfed the radiance of the sun so that every human being would have been awakened by his arrival and over-whelmed by the warmth of his presence. Then he could have ordered his seraphim posse to start up a universal chant and shake the atmosphere with their shouts of his holiness. The ensuing light, heat, and earthquake would certainly have moved all the people on the planet to cover their eyes, tremble in awe, and acknowledge that someone greater than all others had descended on their world.

He could have been born in a palace to a great king and queen. Lived in the most luxurious "crib" ever built. Had silk diapers, cashmere blankets, the purest baby food, gold teething rings—the whole nine yards. But nothing of the sort happened. Jesus took an entirely different approach.

Instead, he came out of Mary's womb to an audience of animals in a small Judean town called Bethlehem. His parents were from

Nazareth, a town in the Galilean backwoods with a reputation for producing nothing good (see John 1:46). His adoptive dad was a blue-collar worker struggling to make an honest shekel, and his mom got pregnant with him before she was married. That had to have had people talking—a pregnant girl "showing" before the wedding. That was not a great situation. To all appearances, Jesus came on the scene like just one more illegitimate child, born into a poor backwoods family, with little hope of doing anything great in his life.

Remember, there was no room for him in the inn. But suppose there had been room in the inn. What if you had been born in a crummy, roach-infested motel on the outskirts of town? Would that be embarrassing to you, or humiliating? Well, Jesus didn't even get that. When he was born, his mother laid him in a manger, a feeding trough for farm animals. We're talking about a place with essentially the same bacteria count as a gas station bathroom. You know, the kind where you flush the toilet with your foot because you're afraid to touch anything with your hands.

Why would Jesus be willing to be born that way? Why would the One with angels created to tell him how great he is come to earth that way, birthed around smelly farm animals and dung droppings? Now God *did* supply angels to make a special announcement to a group of local shepherds, but otherwise the world went on essentially undisturbed. Only some rich guys from the Far East saw any other sign that the glorious One had come to earth. Few people even knew he had come. That just doesn't seem to communicate greatness.

If Jesus' greatness was not revealed in a big way at his birth, then maybe that revelation came during his adult life? The closest we do come to an event where Jesus reveals his glory on earth is the Transfiguration. As Mark 9 records, Jesus took three of his disciples and went up on a mountain, where he was transformed into a figure shining with glorious light. The disciples who were with him fell down in awe and could only stumble for words. They were getting a view of Jesus' true glory and didn't know how to react. At one point Peter even asked if they could build shelters for Jesus and his two glorious companions, Moses and Elijah, to inhabit.

For the three disciples, this experience would have been a lot like Isaiah's experience. Is that what Isaiah saw? They got to see God's glory glowing around Jesus and hear the thunderous voice of the Father say, "This is my dearly loved Son. Listen to him" (Mark 9:7).

And we should. But seeing a bit of Jesus' glory for a few moments was different from having him teach the disciples how to be great. All of his miracles—healing the blind, bringing people back to life, walking on water, and casting out demons—showed his greatness, but then Jesus was fully God and fully human. What about giving us humans a chance to be great? Where was the recipe for greatness?

The friends Jesus made and the people he touched showed no signs of having achieved greatness through meeting the right people in places of power and influence. Jesus himself was actually known as a friend of low-life Jews who collected taxes for the oppressive Roman government. He spent time with drunks and prostitutes in his effort to call Israel back to holiness. He did not wine and dine at fancy Roman parties or get chummy with the priests who controlled the Temple and ran the Jewish law courts. His compatriots were anything but great, and he did more to make the famous and powerful leaders of Roman Palestine angry at him than he did to win their respect and honor. So he certainly did not teach us how to be great by working his way up the ancient corporate food chain into a place of authority and prominence.

So if not at his birth and not throughout his life, maybe he would teach us greatness during his final entrance into Jerusalem at the beginning of Passover, just a few days before he died? That would have been a great time to show us. He could have slowly gathered a mass of followers who would all rise up and crown him king when he entered the city. He could have taken a patient and covert approach that waited until enough people recognized his greatness before he called on them to declare it publicly in word and deed. In this approach, the disciples could have organized music and choirs. There could have been a Jewish army of 500,000 soldiers and an angelic army of one million, with other followers dressed in fancy robes and carrying banners. All of these could have descended on the city in full battle array with a thousand chariots and great stallions leading the charge. Now that would have been great!

But no such rise to greatness occurred during the Triumphal Entry. Instead of a parade of chariots and stallions leading an army marked by banners proclaiming Jesus' kingship, Jesus came waddling down the Mount of Olives toward Jerusalem on a young donkey. Instead of a band with music echoing through the valley, a crowd of ordinary people came out, shouting his praise and throwing branches and clothes on the ground in front of him. Those with power and influence in Jerusalem gave him no respect, and a few Pharisees even told Jesus to make his little followers stop shouting. Although his small band of followers showed their support, Jesus did not show us how to unleash greatness and ascend to status and prestige at just the right time in one's career. He came to a city where influential people plotted his death.

In our search to find out where Jesus teaches us how to become great, we seem to be running out of time. He didn't seem to show us how to do it when he came on the earthly scene or while growing up here, and he didn't seem to show us how to do it when he arrived at Jerusalem for his final days. Or did he? He certainly had a ministry full of great acts, but he spent most of his time with the poor and rejected elements of the Jewish population instead of working his way up to the top. But now, with only days left before his death, there's another chance. Do you remember? He broke up a conversation among his disciples about who was the greatest, and he dropped a huge bombshell: The last will be first. The humble person is the greatest. Jesus had actually been showing us the whole time, from his birth all the way to this point. But he had been saving a special final lesson for the night before his death. And now for everyone who had missed it being displayed his whole life, he would show us very plainly how to become great.

Getting Down and Dirty

In John 13 we find Jesus around a table with his disciples for the Last Supper. They have all just come in from a day of ministry in the dusty streets of Jerusalem. Their feet are dirty, and there is no servant to wash the filth from them. So Jesus picks up a towel, gets some water, and decides to be the humble servant among his disciples.

Now the other men in that room knew how inappropriate it would be for any of them to touch one another's feet, much less the One who had angels created to praise him! The job of foot washing was saved for the lowest of the low, the servants of the servants. Only the least important, most underprivileged people—those who had been born among a bunch of farm animals or in a gas station bathroom—got stuck with that duty. In fact, rabbinic documents show that rabbis and Pharisees in the time after Christ would force their disciples to serve them in every way that slaves would serve their masters *except* for one thing: They were never, ever to touch anyone's feet. That was simply too demeaning for any "respectable" human being to endure.

So the statement Jesus made by washing his disciples' feet would have been profound. He had said before that greatness came from humbling oneself. He had *said,* "The first shall be last and the last shall be first" (see Matthew 19:30), but now he was *showing* it. He was getting down and dirty. Most kings get served. His greatness would not be achieved by working his way up through the political or religious ranks. He did not try to schmooze powerful people or gather an armed crowd that could rise up against the establishment and make him king. His greatness was being worked out as he went out of his way to serve those around him. In a move that ran counter to his culture, he *descended* to greatness.

Do I Know How to Serve?

When I was twenty-two, I spent a couple of years as an intern under Adrian Despres, an itinerant evangelist with Kingdom Building Ministries and the current chaplain for Steve Spurrier and the University of South Carolina Gamecocks football team. I was under the impression that the internship was designed to help me improve as a speaker. I traveled with Adrian to different speaking events all over the world to see what he could teach me about effective communication.

To my chagrin, I found myself attending a bunch of events for my "speaking internship" but never speaking. Adrian would invite me along, tell me where to sit, and then have me listen to him. Eventually he let me start introducing him before I took my seat, but still I didn't get a chance to speak. I constantly wondered whether I had misunderstood the point of the internship. Did Adrian not know that he was supposed to help me become a better communicator, a professional speaker, and not a better audience member? He did finally carve out a one-minute opening spot where I could share a story before sitting down, but that hardly gave me a chance to warm up before taking my seat.

As I kept tagging along to different events, I became more and more bewildered about how I could learn to improve my communication skills. Instead of speaking and getting his feedback, I got to participate in his strange "rituals" before and after his presentations on stage—offstage actions that I thought had nothing to do with speaking. Sometimes we would arrive early at a camp or a church, and he'd have me set up tables and chairs, maybe even vacuum or volunteer in the kitchen. Adrian was the kind of guy who picked up trash and put away shopping carts that other patrons had left scattered around the parking lot. I tried to remind him that "people get paid to do those jobs," but he didn't much care. He would say, "I know. I just want to help 'em out!" Those "rituals" were part of his approach to life and ministry. Maybe somehow these things were linked to Adrian's speaking ministry.

One day, about a year into my internship, Adrian asked if I

thought my internship was going okay. On the inside I was thinking, *Not really! How in the world can I get better at speaking if I don't speak? Doesn't practice make perfect or something like that?* Of course, I didn't come out and say those things. I just answered his inquiry with an affirmative and waited for an explanation. That's when he said something that I'll never forget: "Before we started this whole thing, I knew you could speak. I didn't know if you could serve."

Adrian's comments changed my life. I wanted to be a great speaker. Adrian wanted me to be great *spiritually.*

Let those words ring in your head for a while, and fill in the blank with whatever you are good at. I know you can organize; I just don't know if you can serve. I know you can set up a network in a day; I just don't know if you can serve. I know you can lead a Bible study and pray in public; I just don't know if you can serve. I know you are good at any number of things; I just don't know if you can serve.

You see, Adrian knew that humility + service = greatness. Prideful people usually don't serve unless they do it out of wrong motives. Do you know how to be last? Let that question sink into your conscience. Let it measure your true greatness. And ask yourself, If someone tested you for the next year on whether or not you were a humble servant, what would that person find? Would you show yourself to be great? Would you imitate Jesus and *descend* to greatness? Or do you have trouble taking a backseat and being last?

I Came to Serve

Jesus' ultimate act of humility is described in a poetic formula that Paul likely borrowed from a first-century hymn. The song tells the story of Jesus in his glory making the tough choice to get down and dirty on earth as a human servant. Paul writes, "Though he was God, he did not think of equality with God as something to cling to. Instead, he gave up his divine privileges; he took the humble position of a slave and was born as a human being. When he appeared in human form, he humbled himself in obedience to God and died a criminal's death on a cross" (see Philippians 2:6-8). What "divine privileges" did he give up? Jesus did not give up his deity. But he did give up his rights to full glory, complete majesty, a sinless environment, and continuous praise. The Greatest gave all that up to be last.

When you think about it, Jesus gave up majesty for a mud hole. He came from a trophy room to a cold, smelly manger and a sickly world. Hollywood's *Cribs* has nothing on the mansion and glory Jesus left behind. He gave up a throne room of perfect peace for a place of conflict, where abuse, criticism, suffering, ridicule, and indescribable pain would follow him for thirty-three years and ultimately take his life.

Paul's words in Philippians 2:6-8 make it clear that Jesus' painful and humble service was no accident. He didn't come expecting to receive glory and the accolades of the world. He knew all along that true greatness lives in the form of lowly service. He knew that the path to success in God's economy required a descent to greatness—an unusual twist in our expectations.

Our culture presumes that being first, richest, hippest, happiest, and most liked is the key to finding joy and contentment, the key to being great. The good life is marked by convenience and freebies. Even the church, in some instances, mistakes a blessed life with an easy and unchallenged life. But Jesus calls us to give up our pretensions of greatness defined by fame, carefree living, or accomplishment. Contrary to popular opinion, greatness is defined by the humble and often hidden actions of a person who has given up on coming out on top. It's consistently putting Jesus and others first. Living a life of greatness is actually walking a difficult path of self-sacrifice and inconvenience, driven by a greater concern for others. A truly *great* person does not need to be served but is bent on serving others. Jesus said it himself: "The Son of Man came not to be served but to serve" (Matthew 20:28).

So now, let us begin the journey of being last and descending to greatness.

2

The Way of Blood

"Being Last" by Living a Life of Mercy

[Jesus said,] "A man was going down from Jerusalem to Jericho, and
fell among robbers, and they stripped him and beat him, and went
away leaving him half dead."

—— LUKE 10:30 (NASB) ——

An unnamed man was on a journey from Jerusalem to Jericho.
From what we know about the land in that area, the trek covered
seventeen miles as the man descended thirty-three hundred feet
from atop the Judean hills down into the Jordan River valley and
Jericho.

That in itself was no stroll in the park. And not only did the
man have to move through the Judean wilderness—marked by
rocky hills, sand, and hot winds—but he also faced the dangers
of life on the road. Outlaws, thieves, and hoodlums hid among
the rocks and hills of the wilderness and made their living by
attacking unprotected travelers. The road from Jerusalem to Jericho became so notorious for highway robbery and killings that it
earned the nickname The Way of Blood.

Besides all that, as we read this story, we must understand
the long history of enmity between the Jews and the Samaritans.

These groups *loathed* each other. The Jews looked down on Samaritans—who were a mix of Jew and Gentile—as unclean, corrupt, half-breeds and wanted nothing to do with them because they were "enemies of God."

Round One: The Priest

By chance a priest was going down on that road, and when he saw him, he passed by on the other side.

LUKE 10:31 (NASB)

As soon as Jesus mentioned the word *priest* in this illustration, his listeners would have instantly recognized one of the most prominent members of society. The priests were mediators between sinful Jews and their holy God. The occupation of priest required strict adherence to rules of ceremonial purity, because God's holiness requires all who would approach him to be holy. If a priest came in contact with unclean or dead people, he became "unclean" (unable to participate in any spiritual or social activities) and had to undertake a long cleansing process before returning to his priestly duties. Unfortunately, priests often used the requirements of their sacred occupation as an excuse not to bother themselves with those they saw as objects of reproach. So let's take a closer look at how this "righteous" priest dealt with the man God placed in front of him.

As the priest travels down the road, he sees the half-dead man and is faced head on with a hefty decision. *Do I reach out and help the guy, who's obviously in need, or do I think of myself? Me or him? Him or me? If I help him, that knocks me off my schedule, especially since I'll have to go through the long and embarrassing ritual of washings to be made ceremonially clean again. I may not be able to accomplish all I planned to do today.*

You know what he chose. He would stay clean and "on time," while the victim was about to flatline.

Jesus' point in this story rings true for every man and woman in every place and time: One's "spirituality" or "religion" should not become an excuse for avoiding opportunities to show compassion. Those who obey Jesus' commands to love their neighbors and to treat others as they themselves desire to be treated do not avoid bloody, hurting, down-and-outers simply because of concern for themselves.

In fact, those who take a backseat, become last, and serve their neighbors in need are rewarded by God in intangible ways that they may never be aware of or recognize this side of heaven. What ways? I don't know for sure. Maybe that old car with 175,000 miles just keeps chugging along. Maybe that aging body remains intact, free of sickness or injury. Maybe that repair bill comes in significantly lower than expected. Maybe an only daughter meets a Christian young man. The possibilities go on, but I think you get my drift.

When we become last, God molds us, fills us, and uses us—our lives, our time, our energy—the way he desires, and we are rewarded in unexpressed as well as inexpressible ways.

Taking the Other Side

When I was growing up in Washington, D.C., I witnessed many people "taking the other side of the road," just like the priest in this parable did. Time and time again I watched men or women spot a homeless person in their path and make the split-second decision to cross the street in order to avoid confrontation. Those men or women may not have had the same "religious" reasons for avoidance as the priest in our story, but they shared the same strategy. I know from firsthand experience how easy it can be to see a need, cross to the other side, and completely erase the event from one's mind within seconds.

Since my early days in ministry, God has placed in my heart a special love for the homeless. In fact, when I was eighteen and got my first shot at preaching, it came in a homeless shelter that required those who stayed there to attend a Christian service before enjoying a warm meal, a shower, and a bed for the night. My friends and I also tried to launch our own homeless ministry one Christmas Day by making a load of sandwiches and delivering them to the homeless of D.C. I remember feeling awkward and scared out there on the streets with the less fortunate.

Once, I was walking down a narrow street, hushed by the nearness of buildings on both sides and veiled in darkness by their shadows. My senses were on alert because I knew that setting provided the seclusion preferred by the homeless. A short way down the road I came upon a man perched atop an industrial building's vent that provided much-needed warmth. "Hey, man," I said, "you want to come down and grab a sandwich or a drink?" I was thinking he could use a moment of celebration on Christmas Day.

I won't record his retort here. But not only did he cuss me out instead of thanking me, he also waved a two-by-four at me and threatened to use it on me if I didn't skedaddle. That experience was not all that uncommon. During my various efforts at homeless ministry, I encountered drug use, fighting, and a lot more cussing. And I learned a good deal about how to make the most of difficult ministry situations.

I remember a time when I thought I was about to learn a lot more from two men I looked up to as devout Christian role models. Along with several other guys, we'd been out for an amazing dinner consisting of cooked-to-order steaks, marinated chicken, an endless salad bar, and desserts from The Cheesecake Factory. As guys can do, we ate too much and went stumbling out of the restaurant with only one remaining craving: nap time!

As we strolled back to the hotel, we came across a homeless man asking for help, and my curiosity kicked in. I was excited to see how the two older gentlemen up front would handle the situation. From the back of the group, I watched those gentlemen—men of the faith—as they heard the request of the homeless man and . . . walked right past him without skipping a beat. They didn't even acknowledge his existence.

I was shocked.

They had shut the homeless man out of their minds as soon as they'd laid eyes on him.

When we got back to our hotel, I broke down in my room and wept. I know people are at different places in their journeys toward living like Christ, but these two heroes of Christianity had just fallen before my eyes. Now maybe they didn't really hear the man. Maybe they were deep in conversation that could not be interrupted. Or maybe like the priest on the other side of the road, their personal agenda weighed more heavily than an act of compassion on behalf of the needy. They didn't cross the street, but they still found a way to avoid the call for compassion. They put themselves first. I'm sure at some point I have done the same thing, setting a weak and pathetic example of avoidance for the people following behind me.

Round Two: The Levite

A Levite also, when he came to the place and saw him, passed by on the other side. LUKE 10:32 (NASB)

Even though the half-dead man in Jesus' story lost round one when the priest dodged him, he got a second chance when a Levite came along. Now, you may ask, "Who or what is a Levite?" If you were one of the people listening to Jesus that day, the mention of a Levite would have immediately made you think about time you'd spent in the Temple.

God had appointed the Levites (the name itself just means that they were from the tribe of Levi) to serve in many different roles within the Temple, from leading music and singing psalms to serving as doorkeepers and organizing sacrifices. So when Jesus introduced the Levite into his story, the people would have recognized this character as a man from a special class of Temple servants—again, a member of the religious elite. And if a Levite had contact with a corpse or unclean person, he, too, would become ceremonially unclean and have the hassle of going through the process of ritual cleansing in order to regain his sanctified status, and he would be unable to serve in the Temple for a time.

Needless to say, he followed the path of the priest and crossed to the other side of the road, an important safety measure, since some Pharisees taught that a person could be defiled if even one's shadow fell on a corpse!

No Excuses

One element of Jesus' story that is often overlooked is the direction the priest and the Levite were heading as they traveled along the road. Scripture specifies that the man who was robbed was "going down from Jerusalem to Jericho" and that the priest was "going down on that road" and so was "a Levite also." If they were going "down on that road," that means they were going to Jericho. And if they were going to Jericho, that means they were not on their way to Jerusalem to serve in the Temple but were traveling away from there for some other purpose.

The point is, even if the traveler had been dead, his "uncleanness" wouldn't have interfered with the priest's or the Levite's role at the Temple; had they helped him, their service to God and Israel would not have been disturbed. What it adds up to is that they cared more about their own spiritual status than about other people's basic needs! They refused to be last!

The religious requirements of their roles were designed to honor God and draw people's attention to him, but these religious leaders failed to do that. They showed concern for themselves instead of concern for the man, all the while pretending that their lack of compassion was a reflection of their obedience to God's law. Now that is not good. Or maybe it's just so close to home that it makes us feel uncomfortable. In any case, where the spiritual elite had failed, the next unexpected pedestrian would succeed.

Round Three: The Samaritan

[Jesus said,] "A Samaritan, who was on a journey, came upon [the man]; and when he saw him, he felt compassion, and came to him and bandaged up his wounds, pouring oil and wine on them; and he put him on his own beast, and brought him to an inn and took care of him. On the next day he took out two denarii and gave them to the innkeeper and said, 'Take care of him; and whatever more you spend, when I return I will repay you.'

"Which of these three [travelers] do you think proved to be a neighbor to the man who fell into the robbers' hands?"

And [the lawyer] said, "The one who showed mercy toward him."

Then Jesus said to him, "Go and do the same."

LUKE 10:33-37 (NASB)

The third and final person to show up on the road was a contrast with the Jewish religious elite. Jesus' choice of a priest and a Levite to precede the final traveler, who would act with compassion, was deliberate. The laws about purity, designed to teach lessons about God's holiness, were used instead as excuses for misrepresenting God's love and compassion. Jesus was making the point that sometimes those who are revered and respected for their religious service can completely miss the heart of God.

Who would this third person in the story be? Was the audience thinking of a Jewish blue-collar citizen or someone else they could relate to? Maybe a Jewish farmer, fisherman, merchant, or carpenter like Jesus? To make his point, Jesus throws a huge curveball: He picks a person from the most disdained and disrespected class of people—the Samaritans—to turn the Jewish "religious" community on its ear.

When Jesus mentioned "a certain Samaritan," the crowd may have fallen silent, their inquisitive expressions turning into frowns of disgust. Once the shock had subsided, people intently following the story may have expected Jesus to talk about how the Samaritan took advantage of the half-dead Jew, or how the Samaritan was really the assailant who came back and finished him off. They may have been thinking, *How could a half-breed Samaritan who worships at the wrong temple do anything better than a holy priest and a committed Levite?* They probably feared that the Samaritan would defile the bloody Jew rather than the other way around, because Jews *hated* Samaritans. They didn't want to talk to them, live near them, or even travel through the land where they lived. In the Jews' opinion, Samaritans had corrupted the faith once delivered by Moses and had defiled themselves with the Gentiles.

Jesus knew all of those thoughts. He'd grown up in that segregated region and encountered its prejudices and racism firsthand. When he decided to put a Samaritan in his story, he knew that it would elicit the full attention of the Jews. Indeed, he had set his audience up for a most surprising twist: The Samaritan did the traveler no harm—in fact, he did the opposite! The text says that "he felt compassion, and came to him." Where the priest and Levite moved away from the injured man, the Samaritan—of all people—moved toward him.

That is what true servanthood is all about. Not only does your heart go out to someone in need, but humility takes over, compassion kicks in, you forget yourself and your circumstances, and your actions become those of a servant. While the religious elite were overcome by an internal concern for themselves, the Samaritan was overwhelmed by a compassion that made him blind to any harm that might come to him for helping.

How do you descend to greatness? Look at the Samaritan. He was last in the world's eyes. Yet he humbly took his own wine and oil to clean and disinfect the man's wounds. It was a sacrifice. He bandaged the man, hoisted him onto his own animal (which meant he would have to walk), and took him to the nearest inn. Once they had arrived, the Samaritan spent the night tending to the beaten man. The next day he left two denarii to cover further expenses required for the man to stay and recover, promising to pay more, if necessary, when he returned! What the Samaritan did was show a radical, selfless investment in the life and health of a man he did not even know—a man who was likely a social enemy, a Jew. The Good Samaritan was the perfect contrast to the religious elite, who had lost the heart of God in the midst of their religious service. It was as if the Samaritan was walking through life, alert and sensitive, just waiting to be led by God into some new, unpredictable situation in which he could demonstrate the love and compassion of God. He was ready and willing to be last.

His actions were remarkable.

Are you like him?

Are you willing to be last?

What Do You Care?

I venture to guess that virtually everyone reading this book would say, "I care about people." But because the purpose of this book is to help us look into the mirror of God's Word and find out what we are *really* like, I need to ask this question: How do you know you care about people? In other words, where's the proof?

The answer should be simple.

You put others first!

If you frequently *take action* to help people in need, then chances are you have compassion. You care about people. If you find yourself lending your car or pickup truck, letting a single mom stay in your basement apartment for free, sponsoring a child through Compassion International, purchasing a gift for a friend you've been witnessing to, stopping on the side of the road to help a stranded elderly couple, or teaching a former juvenile delinquent how to hold down a job and budget his money, then yes, you do care about those in need. Your compassion is real because it moves you to take action.

I know a guy who used to keep a box or two of Wheat Thins crackers in his car, not only to snack on but also for the times when he would pull up to a stoplight at the end of an exit ramp and see a homeless man or woman asking for money to buy food. Along with a few dollars, he'd offer the Wheat Thins. Better yet, whenever possible, he took that person out for a meal. That gave him the chance to meet a physical need and also discover how he might point that person to the ultimate need—a living relationship with Jesus.

One of my most humbling encounters occurred in a Subway restaurant near the part of downtown Denver that attracts homeless teenagers. One night a homeless, hungry teenage boy asked me for some food. After we had eaten a meal together and talked about Jesus, he knelt on the sidewalk, skateboard in hand, and prayed with me. He asked God to forgive his sins. God used one Subway sandwich and an hour's time out of my schedule to give that young man a chance to redirect his life.

Sometimes I don't have time to take someone out for a meal and don't have any food in the car, so I give money. When I tell people that, they immediately start naming all of the ways the recipient could misuse the money (buying alcohol or cigarettes, for example). But I don't give away *my* money; I give them *Jesus'* money (and I'm not talking about the tract most of us have seen that looks like money but isn't!).

Before I give away any money, I try to say something like this: "Hey, man, I'm a Christian. And I think Jesus wants me to give you some of his money, which he actually gave me first. Everything I have comes from Jesus, so why don't you take some of his money, get something to eat, do something good with it, and thank him for how much he loves you. See ya."

Is that naive? I don't know, but I would rather err on the side of giving than of keeping.

Do the people who take the money always do something good with it? Do they buy drugs and alcohol? Do they spend it on a meal or a couple of new shirts from the thrift store? I don't know. But I do know that in that moment, I was called to demonstrate the compassion of Jesus. Action was required from me, and the rest was up to God. The way I look at it, Jesus helped them out, and they had a responsibility to act accordingly.

What about you? Do you move away from the needy in your heart and in your actions, or do you move *toward* them? Do you care about people, or has your religion morphed into an excuse to avoid the hurting while you focus on your own spiritual status? These are wise questions to ponder. They can be answered definitively and can help you avoid any self-deception. Simply think about how many people you have gone out of your way to help in the past year, and you have your answer—because actions don't lie.

The fact is, Jesus measures the goodness of a soul not by a heart that is feasting on its own spirituality but by a heart that is moved to compassion and then to action.

When we become last, we become free:

+ free of time restraints and "to do" lists
+ free of self-serving habits, trivial obligations, and suffocating selfishness
+ free to see a need and respond

Where are you on the road to becoming a free agent of Jesus?

3

We Got Caught—
He Got Punished

"Being Last" by Living a Life of Sacrifice

Before we go any further in our discussion of what this lifestyle of being last means, we have to understand one critical point: Being last is not drudgery. It's not a pain in the neck. It's not a yoke. If it is, something's wrong. Being last is a joyful, meek, thankful, fulfilling way of life that God bestows on us as we realize what Jesus Christ has done for us at the cross.

My friend Mark told of a shocking statistic from the 2000 census that struck a chord deep in my heart. Out of the 290 million people who live in the United States, one person dies every 15 seconds. That means about 4 people die every minute, 240 people every hour, and 5,760 every day. On paper, it's easy to dismiss these numbers as cold statistics, but for Mark, they are what fuel his unbridled passion for evangelism. Mark recognizes that people are dying all around him, every minute of every day, and that there is something he can do—something his "be last" lifestyle can trigger—that can alter people's eternal destiny.

Why Die?

As I get older and experience more of this crazy journey called life, I realize that hardship is part of the program. Death is part of life. We lose loved ones, sometimes after long, full lives; other times, tragically, after only weeks, or days, or even hours of life. And ultimately, we must face death too.

Whew!

The fact of death is a cold, hard truth that has the potential either to steer people away from God or to draw them closer to him. The concept of "death to self" plays an integral role in being last. So as we delve into the dynamic impact the "last" lifestyle can have on those around us, it's vital that we understand why people die. Otherwise, we're trying to offer an explanation of, and solution to, a problem we don't understand. Genesis 3 gives us what we need. We'll jump into the story just after God created Adam and Eve and instructed them about life in the Garden:

> The serpent was the shrewdest of all the wild animals the LORD God had made. One day he asked the woman, "Did God really say you must not eat the fruit from any of the trees in the garden?"
>
> "Of course we may eat fruit from the trees in the garden," the woman replied. "It's only the fruit from the tree in the middle of the garden that we are not allowed to eat. God said, 'You must not eat it or even touch it; if you do, you will die.'"
>
> "You won't die!" the serpent replied to the woman. "God knows that your eyes will be opened as soon as you eat it, and you will be like God, knowing both good and evil."
>
> The woman was convinced. She saw that the tree was beautiful and its fruit looked delicious, and she wanted the wisdom it would give her. So she took some of the fruit and ate it. Then she gave some to her husband, who was with her, and he ate it, too. GENESIS 3:1-6

These six verses provide the timeless picture of humanity's great turning point. We had an open, obedient relationship with God. The rules for living were clear and concise. And in that perfectly created world that God had given us to manage and enjoy, the possibilities of life and happiness were endless. Yet we succumbed to the self-centered admonitions and trappings of a cruel, deceptive serpent.

Although I can't explain why a woman ventured into a conversation with a snake, I can attest to how crafty that serpent became during their conversation. First, by exaggerating God's instructions, he *questioned* whether or not God had really prohibited Adam and Eve from eating any fruit in the Garden: "Did God really say you must not eat the fruit from any of the trees in the garden?" (v. 1).

Second, he *challenged* God's declaration that death would result: "You won't die!" the serpent hissed (v. 4). And finally, the serpent had the audacity to *change* the consequences from death, which God had outlined, to power and knowledge: "You will be like God, knowing both good and evil" (v. 5). With each statement, Satan undermined God's authority and disguised the true consequences that would result from eating the fruit. Unfortunately, his scheme worked: The man and woman rebelled.

Perhaps you're asking yourself, *Was it really that big a deal for Eve and Adam to eat some fruit?* That's a good question, especially because no other drastic, rebellious behavior is recorded. No other sin. It's not as if Eve murdered Adam. She didn't steal from him. He didn't lie to her. There was no cheating or any other outrageous behavior recorded. They just decided to eat a piece of fruit. So why did it change the future and destroy humanity's perfect relationship with God?

29

The answer can be summed up in one word: holiness—or, more specifically, God's holiness. Because God is holy, anything that goes against his perfect way is sin, and his character will not allow him to tolerate it. If he did, he would be contradicting himself and permitting imperfection with all its destructive consequences. Adam and Eve's choice to eat the fruit was contrary to God's perfect command to them, so there must be punishment. God had already told them what the consequence of disobedience would be. That's why he says in Genesis 3:19, "You were made from dust, and to dust you will return"; in other words, Adam and Eve would have to die. The apostle Paul put it this way: "The wages of sin is death" (Romans 6:23). Sinful human beings must die.

God's instructions to refrain from eating the fruit from one tree provided a simple test to make sure humanity would respectfully follow his perfect ways. The test could have been anything, but the response would have needed to be the same. Keep in mind that it was *only one tree* that they had to stay away from, just one. They had the entire Garden. I wonder how many trees there were. Hundreds to choose from? Maybe thousands? It was almost as if God were making it hard for them to sin because he loved them so much. They needed to stay away from just one tree to continue in their perfect relationship with God. They needed to acknowledge that he was holy and right, and their simple obedience—even in the face of their own curiosity—would have allowed them to pass the test. But they did sin. Adam and Eve clearly showed who they thought should be in charge and whose desires should come first. So, in one small act of consumption they made a grand declaration of independence from God, and he was forced to respond justly.

The result—an across-the-board sentence of death—now plagues every one of us: "Each person is destined to die once and after that comes judgment" (Hebrews 9:27). It might be in fifty years, and it might be in fifty days. But unless Jesus comes back first, we all have a date with death, a date that will be engraved on our tombstones.

Don't Do the Crime If You Can't Do the Time

Do you remember what it felt like to get caught doing something wrong and know that you would have to face the consequences? Maybe you even felt fine about what you were doing—right up until you got caught. I remember such an incident. I was a teenager, it was five in the morning, and I was attempting to sneak back into my parents' house undetected.

Back then, my parents didn't have a whole lot of money. I drove a 1982 Pontiac Bonneville, which, I believe, must have been an LTE (Limited "Tank" Edition), because I had heard that transportation engineers were discussing widening the roads just so the car could stay between the lines. The engine had developed an unmistakable roar, which made trying to get home unnoticed extremely difficult. Needing a stealthy approach, I decided to shut down the engine a few blocks away from the house and coast the Bonneville into the driveway.

After nearly destroying family property on the way into the driveway with the weaving, gas-guzzling "tank," I breathed a sigh of relief as I eased the car to a stop. I'd made it! I tiptoed through the door, chuckling to myself, and headed for my room, only to find my father sitting in a chair across the living room. As he rose to his feet, my every hope was dashed, and guilt and regret engulfed me. Standing tall, like a man, I prepared to hand over my license and face whatever punishment Dad felt would help me learn to be responsible. That was a very scary moment for me.

Death Sentence

A man named Barabbas faced a much greater consequence for his crime. His life was also on the line when Pilate attempted to release Jesus in order to escape controversy. Barabbas was *not* someone you'd want to bump into in a dark alley:

> One of the prisoners . . . was Barabbas, a revolutionary who had committed murder in an uprising.   MARK 15:7

Some scholars believe that Barabbas belonged to a gang called the *Sicarii,* a political terrorist cell that was bent on bringing an end to Roman rule in Judea. The Sicarii were known for carrying daggers *(sicae)* that were small enough to conceal under their clothing but big enough to do major damage in a fight. Barabbas himself might have used such a weapon when he committed murder during the uprising. At any rate, he apparently did not conceal his actions well enough and was caught by the Roman government.

Barabbas had no hope of an easy or temporary punishment. The penal system had no probationary period in which good behavior might earn him a lesser sentence. There was no appeals process to give him a chance to find a loophole in the law. He had no recourse as he sat in his prison cell. When the Romans were ready to carry out the crucifixions, he would be one of the next in line to be marched out to the hill where his hands and feet would be pierced, his shoulders would be ripped out of their sockets, and he would die a slow and agonizing death by asphyxiation. It was a reality he had to accept.

Guilty!

Barabbas would likely have been kept in a holding chamber of what was called Antonia Fortress. This fortress stood adjacent to the Temple grounds, about one-third of a mile from Pilate's quarters, where Jesus' latest trial was unfolding. At this stage of the trial, Pilate, wanting to avoid any further unrest, gave the Jews a chance to ask for the release of one prisoner, either Jesus the Messiah or Barabbas the murderer. But his attempt to persuade the crowd to ask for Jesus' release failed:

> The leading priests and the elders persuaded the crowd to ask for Barabbas to be released and for Jesus to be put to death. So the governor asked again, "Which of these two do you want me to release to you?"
> The crowd shouted back, "Barabbas!"
> MATTHEW 27:20-21

I have to wonder whether the roar of the crowd could be heard down the street in the cells of the Antonia Fortress. If so, what was Barabbas thinking when he heard echoes of his name? Did he think they were crying for his imminent death? Was his mind filled with horror as he prepared to be crucified in front of a hostile crowd that would be entertained by his suffering?

Back at the trial, Pilate responded to the crowd's decision: "'Then what should I do with Jesus who is called the Messiah?' They shouted back, 'Crucify him!'" (Matthew 27:22). Imagine how the merciless shouts of those demanding death penetrated the dark spaces of the fortress and brought more terror to the condemned murderer. First, he'd heard his name. Now, cries for crucifixion. A life's worth of thoughts must have raced through his frazzled mind as he slumped in the corner of his cell and thought, *It's over.*

An Unforgettable Scene

Try to picture this moment in time: Through the dust, heat, and terror you can see two men. One is sentenced to die for murder; the other is sentenced to die because he offended the wrong crowd. One sits brimming with hatred, fear, and anger; the other, wrongly accused, stands before the people he loves, only to be mocked and ridiculed. One deserves death; the other has the power of life and death over every screaming person in front of him. One will walk out of the city a free man; the other will walk out of the city to a hill called the Skull, where he will be tortured to death. The inequity is heartbreaking. But the story is true.

Think about what Barabbas might have experienced moments later: A captain at the Antonia Fortress receives a message ordering Barabbas's immediate release. He sends a soldier down the stairs to pull the prisoner out of his cell. Barabbas retches at the sound of the guard's footsteps. He hears keys rattle, the gate opening, and then these words: "Barabbas, as an act of ceremonial benevolence on the part of Pontius Pilate, you shall go free today."

Whoa! Talk about mind blowing. What went through Barabbas's mind when he heard those words? Can you imagine the utter relief? His sin had warranted judgment and death, but in an instant, he received an undeserved pardon and a whole new start. None of his nightmares would come true. Just thinking about the reprieve puts a lump in my throat. That God could arrange such a drastic display of his love for that sinful man is simply amazing.

I wonder what occurred after his release. Once Barabbas was let out of the fortress, did he end up in the crowd lining the streets as Jesus was led in the direction of Golgotha? The scene would have been unforgettable. A bruised, bloody man drags himself and his cross down the street, enduring the lash of a whip at every sign of slowing. The crowd harasses him, spits, and throws rocks. Perhaps Barabbas is even in on the fun.

What impact did it have on Barabbas to know that another man was to suffer the torture he himself deserved? Did he chase after Jesus in gratitude? Did he seek to learn more about Jesus' life and message? Or did he just mock and spit like all the rest? There are conflicting legends that attempt to answer whether or not Barabbas devoted his life to Jesus after being freed. So we will not know how he reacted until we get to heaven.

Our Date with Destiny

Did Barabbas become a Christian, or didn't he? And what's the big deal, anyway? He was still going to die someday. His date with death had only been postponed. The real issue, of course, is not when or how he would die but what would happen to him *after* he died. Would he be welcomed into heaven by Jesus, who had died in his place, or would everlasting torment in hell begin the moment after his death? His decision, though unknown to us, determined his destiny. And your decision will determine yours.

Maybe you're unsure about what that "decision" really looks like in your life. Or, perhaps you think you know about the decision, but the Bible actually teaches something different. In either case, numerous passages within the Scriptures provide a full picture of the authentic life and heart change that warrants salvation. A succinct view of the process is given by the apostle Paul in 2 Corinthians: "The kind of sorrow God wants us to experience leads us away from sin and results in salvation. There's no regret for that kind of sorrow. But worldly sorrow, which lacks repentance, results in spiritual death" (7:10). Now let's take a closer look at Paul's focus on repentance and sorrow.

Godly Sorrow and Repentance

Repentance (turning) begins with the realization that our lives are full of sin and vileness and rebellion. We start to see how we've hurt others, savored evil, twisted the truth, lived for ourselves, and slandered and undermined our authorities. We face the fact that although others may appear to be worse than we are, *we* still have major problems. We serve ourselves first, and in doing so, we harm those around us. And we cannot change on our own.

By God's grace, that is, his undeserved favor, we become disgusted with our lifestyle and begin to ask, "What is the meaning of life?" Finally, we recognize that just like Adam and Eve and Barabbas, we have offended God, who created us to be righteous. And that knowledge leads us to sorrow.

Godly sorrow leads us to an overwhelming sense of the sickening, insensitive, hypocritical approach we've taken in life. It weighs deeply on our hearts and may even express itself through tears and anguish. We now feel sorry because of how much our sins have hurt God—the One who paid so much for our freedom. We even begin to understand that our sin caused his physical pain: "He was pierced for our rebellion, crushed for our sins. He was beaten so we could be whole. He was whipped so we could be healed" (Isaiah 53:5).

The cold, stark facts become so personal that they may make us drop to the floor in pain and heartache. Sorrow has come on a level we've rarely, if ever, experienced. In the midst of that pain, however, God gives us the humility, motivation, and supernatural power to turn away (repent) from that lifestyle, to say, "Thank you for your grace and mercy, God. Thank you for rescuing me from the hellish fate I deserved! Thank you for bending my heart toward you." *That* is the sorrow that leads to repentance, to an internal and external change that characterizes salvation.

My Hands, His Suffering

Recently, I learned an interesting fact about Mel Gibson's movie *The Passion of the Christ.* You may have seen this film, which graphically portrays the final hours of Jesus' earthly life. Although I do not believe the movie is a 100 percent accurate representation of the facts (since it was one group's interpretation of the events), the details of Jesus' physical suffering probably match the historical reality better than any film to date. So I applaud Mel Gibson's efforts to bring Christ's sacrifice and ministry to life in the minds and hearts of so many.

In a prime-time interview, Gibson revealed that he'd made an appearance in the movie, although his face was never shown on the big screen. That struck me as odd until he explained. The cameo occurred while Christ was being nailed to the cross. With the musical score reverberating and Jesus lying bloody on the cross, it is Gibson's hands that drive the spikes into Jesus' hands and feet. When asked why he chose to use his own hands, he said that he was personally responsible, along with the rest of the world, for the crucifixion.

His statement could not be truer. Christ's pain came from *our* sin. Like Barabbas and like Adam and Eve, we deserve death and punishment for our sinful nature. Jesus took our place. He rescued us.

Perhaps you've become callous to your sins. Maybe you don't think that you're *that* bad. You may even have lied to yourself, thinking your dark habits have been successfully hidden. But although you may have tried to deceive yourself, the Scriptures say that "the LORD is watching everywhere, keeping his eye on both the evil and the good" (Proverbs 15:3).

God sees our sin. We are caught. And he is watching with eyes full of love and hands full of scars. Remember his words when he was being beaten and spit upon? "Father, forgive them, for they don't know what they are doing" (Luke 23:34). Our sin spits in God's face, yet he is quick to forgive. He has no desire that we see our sin and then sink into depression. Instead, he wants us to recognize that he took the consequences so we could receive a new life. He took our punishment so that we could experience the highest form of human life: a relationship with our loving Creator.

How then should we live? Paul wrote, "Dear brothers and sisters, I plead with you to give your bodies to God because of all he has done for you. Let them be a living and holy sacrifice—the kind he will find acceptable. This is truly the way to worship him" (Romans 12:1).

Every insult, every lash of the whip, every swing of the rod, every bruise and laceration, every thorn ripping into his skull, every nail that pierced his flesh—all of these he endured because of sin, yours and mine.

Jesus suffered what you and I should suffer.

Why did he do it?

Love.

How can I thank him?

Be last and put him first.

Be a vibrant, living, holy sacrifice—and see what Jesus does with a vessel that has been surrendered completely for his use!

4

Love Is Last

"Being Last" by Living a Life of Love

As we'll find out in this chapter, there's something about "being last" that generates within us a Christlike love so powerful and contagious that it has the potential to sweep others away in its current. But it has taken me a long time to realize that.

Back in my college days, I learned a lot in the dorms. When men from around the nation and world—each with his own individual tastes, background, beliefs, and worldview—live under one roof in a college dormitory, it's often a recipe for disaster. Those individual differences can quickly become dangerous. Let me tell you about one such experience.

Bulldog

In the early nineties, when I was in college, I met some unforgettable characters in the halls of the men's dorms. The first guy I encountered seemed confused—not about life in general but about which college he was attending. Everything he owned was decked out in the red and black colors of the University of Georgia, which was a problem because we didn't attend that university—or even one in the state of Georgia!

His dorm room, covered wall to wall with UGA's bulldog mascot, looked like a dog pound. His closet was packed with clothes he'd probably purchased at the UGA bookstore. And every conversation he took part in somehow ended with "Go Dawgs!" Each day he donned a thick, black Bulldog jacket and headed off to class, proudly showing his allegiance despite the warm temperatures that caused him to soak it with sweat. I'm certain he would have housed a fat, slobbering bulldog in his room if pets had been allowed. He was a prime example of why the most devout sports spectators have become known as "fans" (short for "fanatics").

Interestingly, my Bulldog buddy's personality did not reflect the overbearing zeal with which he supported his home team. On the contrary, he was an unusually meek guy who seemed to process life deeply but felt no need to share his thoughts with anyone around him. He was actually very quiet, which seemed odd to me.

I can still remember one of the first times he really opened up to us. We were gathered in a small group, going around the circle and sharing prayer requests. When we got to him, his countenance fell. The rest of us were on the edge of our seats, eager to hear what was weighing so heavily on him. It wasn't the upcoming Bulldogs game. He looked at us, blinked, and said, "Guys, I'd really like for you to pray about the youth group I'm leading."

Wondering if there might be something more specific he wanted to talk about, one of the guys asked, "What exactly do you want us to pray about for your youth group?"

"Well," he replied, looking down as he spoke, "I have one youth . . ." There was a long pause. We all wanted to know more details about what this youth was going through. Then he finished, "And . . . that's all."

It was difficult not to laugh.

But that moment was a window into the Bulldog's soul: *He loved people.*

It didn't matter that his ministry was small at the time. He cared and wanted us to cry out with him for this one soul he was mentoring.

Military Man

One of the next guys I recall from dorm life was cut from a totally different cloth and had a totally different approach to life (although his and the Bulldog's paths would ultimately cross). He had ventured down from Chicago after finishing his tour of duty in Desert Storm. He was a soldier, a true military man. As a member of the 82nd Airborne Division, he had endured thirty-hour land battles from behind the controls of armored vehicles and had made so many flight jumps that he could hardly keep track of them.

When Military Man entered the service, he was given a Gideon Bible as a gift. Although he really didn't want the thing, he found a way to use it after being assigned to the 82nd Airborne Division. Before every jump, Military Man took out the Bible and rubbed it for good luck. After each successful jump he scratched a mark on the inside of the cover and then put the Bible away until the next jump.

During his tenure in the armed forces, Military Man lived an unencumbered lifestyle, getting drunk at every opportunity and living on the edge. When it came to the Bible, he wasn't looking for anything more than a little luck and a handy record book. But he did love to read and once told me that he'd read probably a thousand books in his lifetime. Then one day he decided to use the Gideon Bible he'd been given as more than a good luck charm: He decided to use it as a book.

It wasn't long before Military Man had read the Bible cover to cover. Although he didn't understand all the details, the main message had become clear to him. When he got to the end, he was ready to pray the prayer printed in the back of the Bible. (Those of us who complain about the ineffectiveness of tracts and handouts should make note of this story!) So he prayed the prayer, and his relationship with God began. An overwhelming feeling of being forgiven and an uplifting sense of purpose gave Military Man a new lease on life. In fact—get this—to celebrate his new relationship with Christ, he bought a six-pack and drank for joy. Of course, he would later learn that life is best lived with self-control and a clear mind, but at that moment, it was the only way he knew to express his excitement. I guess in some strange way he was joining the celebration of the angels as they rejoiced over his repentance.

After he had finished his time in the service, he showed up at Bible college, ready to be trained for service in God's army, and he brought with him the same military mentality and discipline that had made him successful in the 82nd Airborne: He was going to study his Bible, learn ancient languages, and prepare for ministry. He knew serving God was serious business, and he was preparing accordingly. He didn't want to waste time on anything other than the most pertinent training exercises—not even relationships. After all, he had a job to do for God, and he didn't want people to get in the way.

Somehow, in the providence—and perhaps, humor—of God, the disciplined Military Man and the friendly Georgia Bulldog ended up on the same hall in the dormitory. The Bulldog was ready to meet and minister to everyone in sight. The Military Man was ready to study in confinement, graduate, and go wherever God deployed him. Needless to say, their "relationship" hit a wall.

Whenever Bulldog tried to drop by and hang out with Military Man, things got rocky. Military Man used every tactic in his arsenal to discourage Bulldog. He ignored him. He wore camouflage. He locked Bulldog out. He didn't even care that his rejection was stone-cold obvious. Soon, Bulldog realized that an even more persistent approach was required. That's when he observed that his unsociable friend often left his door unlocked when he went to class.

One day Military Man returned to the dorm with his usual focused demeanor, made a beeline for his room, and found the Bulldog, decked out in his black UGA jacket, sitting there. Military Man promptly made it clear that he saw no need to waste time shooting the breeze when there was work and training to be done. He was focused on studying the Bible, figuring out his spiritual gifts, and getting out in the field to serve.

But like all faithful pets, Bulldog hung around. And after several more surprise visits, Military Man finally exploded, ordered Bulldog to leave and not come back, and told him to tell everyone else that he didn't want to be disturbed. He even threw in a couple of choice words to get his point across. Undeterred by the outburst, Bulldog wasn't about to let his efforts end without one last, genuine plea from the heart. Looking back at Military Man, he said, "I just care about you, man. And I believe in you. . . . That's it."

The words came down like a hard rain on a rampaging forest fire.

The heat of Military Man's anger turned to the calm of epiphany.

Bulldog's words—combined with his previous efforts to connect with Military Man—changed everything. The two soon became friends, and the rest of the guys on that floor became his friends too. By the end of the school year, Military Man had learned firsthand about the utter importance of relationships and genuine love in ministry. He began to read God's Word in a whole new light—the light of being last, taking the time to listen, and caring enough to love.

Gifts Are Good, but Love Is Better

You may already be familiar with the well-known "love" chapter in the Bible, 1 Corinthians 13, the text of which is read aloud at many weddings. But have you ever taken a look at the chapters that come before and after the love chapter and thought about the placement of those chapters?

Interestingly, the entire discussion in chapters 12 and 14 centers on spiritual gifts. The apostle Paul is talking about how the Spirit of God energizes his people to function in complementary yet distinct roles. Paul's insight is designed to strengthen the whole community. He compares the concept of spiritual gifts to the parts of a human body and the fact that each part functions for the overall betterment and smooth operation of the entire body. Paul asserts that everyone in the body of Christ has a part to play, and he implies that a mere 10 to 20 percent of the people shouldn't be doing all the work. So everyone is needed to do his or her part, whether that part is big or small, up front or behind the scenes.

As Paul communicates how each member can contribute meaningfully to the health of the whole body, he singles out several gifts that were being displayed in more controversial manners. He apparently addressed these particular gifts because a few people who were using these gifts were disturbing those around them. Paul introduced these more controversial gifts in chapter 12 and carefully analyzed them in chapter 14, with the supreme goal of teaching the believers they were to use their gifts not primarily for the spiritual enjoyment of each individual but for the spiritual benefit of the entire community.

Paul's unflinching aim in 1 Corinthians 12–14 was to restore the Corinthian community to health—and a community is healthy only when God is energizing different people with unique gifts and talents to accomplish greater Christian maturity among its members. In 1 Corinthians 12:8-10 and 12:28-30, Paul lists a variety of gifts that have the potential to complement each other with a powerful spiritual dynamic. Yet while discussing this, Paul pauses. Yes, he is convinced that a community of Jesus' followers function best when they find a way for all the parts to work together, but *how* do they actually do that? How do so many different people—with so many different hang-ups and personality traits and selfish desires and ugly faults and different giftings—get along with one another?

Paul pauses in 1 Corinthians 13 to announce that there is one requirement—one undeniable essential—that takes priority over deciphering gifts and finding one's role in the body. In order to fine-tune the functionality of the Corinthian community, Paul couldn't stop at describing the spiritual gifts, at encouraging people to get involved, or even at tempering the use of showy gifts. He knew people and human nature, and he knew he needed to insert some indispensable wisdom about the foundation of the church and the glue that holds God's people together.

Let me show you a way of life that is best of all.

1 CORINTHIANS 12:31

The English expression "best of all" comes from a Greek phrase, *kata hyperbol*, which is used in contexts of comparison where one item is compared to another and demonstrates itself to be on a wholly superior level. The better of the two items is called *kata hyperbolē* because it exceeds the standard by which both items are measured. The better item is essentially "beyond measure" or "beyond ordinary expectations." In other words, we might understand Paul to be describing this "best of all" way as *hands-down, without-a-doubt, superior.* So, what is it that Paul has deemed extraordinary or "off the charts"? What is it that is even more vital than diversely gifted people functioning cooperatively in their individual roles?

It's love. Love is the key.

Without love, special gifts are worthless. Without love, there really isn't much purpose in figuring out one's gift. Love is where it's at. And what does the *hands-down, without-a-doubt-superior* way of love look like to the apostle Paul? He describes it in 1 Corinthians 13:

Love is patient and kind. Love is not jealous or boastful or proud or rude. It does not demand its own way. It is not irritable, and it keeps no record of being wronged. It does not rejoice about injustice but rejoices whenever the truth wins out. Love never gives up, never loses faith, is always hopeful, and endures through every circumstance.

1 CORINTHIANS 13:4-7

Would it be appropriate to say that to love like that, you've got to be last? I think so.

It's Not about Us

Are you familiar with the name game? It's the game in which people try to make a name for themselves. It's a game in which people are so concerned about being viewed as special that they spend their lives scouting out every possible means to show the world what they've got. Somehow they find a way to redirect every conversation back to themselves, their lives, their businesses, their families, or their prowess. They end up looking like some of today's NBA stars who beat their chests every time they make a basket or block a shot because their emotions are so completely wrapped up in the desire to show off *their* stuff and "make a name" for themselves. You know the kind, right?

Let's hold on a minute, though. Before we point a finger at "those" people, we need to take a long look in a mirror. Sometimes I wonder how many of us Christians have, consciously or unconsciously, played a "Christianized" version of the name game. The Christianized version can take on a life of its own. We may not boast about physical strength, supreme intellect, or smooth business deals, but we find ways to tout our impressive "giftedness," flaunt "God's blessings," boast about someone we "witnessed to," or make mention of our admirable "quiet time" and "spiritual growth." And because none of these attributes is bad in and of itself, the game goes on.

But in those arrogant moments when we draw attention to ourselves while trying to prove how important and impressive we are, we can easily slap a Christian label on what we've just done, and no one can call us on it. It's like gossiping under the guise of taking prayer requests. Our language and the things we boast about may be different from the world's, but the game is the same. It's the name game. Is that Jesus' way? Does he want us flaunting our name under the guise of "spirituality"? Or have we simply opted to ignore the *hands-down, without-a-doubt-superior* way of love?

What We Learn from Loving Ourselves

Most of us, with or without realizing it, seek opportunities to show off our stuff. And most of us react in disappointment or even anger when we fail to prove our abilities. These are instincts no human lacks. We naturally pursue what we think makes life best for us, and we react negatively when someone or something gets in the way. The inclination to love ourselves is so strong that Jesus even taps into it in an attempt to help us understand how we're supposed to love others.

> Love others as well as you love yourself.
>
> MATTHEW 22:39 *(The Message)*

Right about now, you may be thinking, "Wait a minute, Jeremy. I don't love myself that much." You might even conclude that God's standard—to love others as well as yourself—is one of the easier commands. If that's you—now don't get upset at me—I would venture to say that you are fooling yourself. Because we are descendants of Adam and Eve, watching out for "me, myself, and I" comes naturally to us 24-7. We do it unconsciously, and if I listed all the ways we do it, I'd have to turn this book into a multivolume set. If you're not sure how selfish you are, ask a friend or family member to be honest with you about the ways in which you tend to cater to yourself day in and day out.

I'm not saying it's wrong for us to take care of ourselves. Jesus doesn't command us to love others and neglect our own needs. He just knows that most of us don't need to be taught to look out for ourselves! We *do*, however, need to be taught to love *others*, and Jesus says we can use our natural instincts to learn how.

So if you want to hone your ability to love others as Christ desires, sit down for a few minutes and reflect on the last five things you did to make yourself feel good. Ask yourself these questions:

+ How have I defended my own reputation today?
+ What was the last desire I fulfilled?
+ Whose needs were most important in the last decision I made?

Your answers to those questions will give you insight about how you're doing at being last and genuinely loving people instead of relegating them to the place of meaningless background images in the painting of your life.

Chase Love, Make It Yours

If we want to love, we need to *initiate it*. Since we're naturally bent on looking out for ourselves, we must fight against that dominating tendency and make strides toward informing ourselves about the other people in the room, in the office, or in the home. The Bible tells us,

> Don't be selfish; don't try to impress others. Be humble, think-
> ing of others as better than yourselves. Don't look out only for
> your own interests, but take an interest in others, too.
>
> PHILIPPIANS 2:3-4

These verses are talking about being last. That may mean consci-
entiously starting every conversation with several questions about
how the other person is doing instead of presenting a monologue
on our own lives. It may mean asking people what's already on
their plates instead of rushing to dump our problems and com-
plaints on them. It will likely even mean doing things that don't
benefit us in any perceivable way. No matter what it means to
you, it requires initiative. If we're going to imitate Christ in loving people, we shouldn't pray and ask him for opportunities to do
so and then go about our days the same old way. We must initiate.
Jesus wouldn't have commanded us to love if loving happened
automatically. We've got to go after it.

Paul makes this point when he moves back and forth from
his lesson on love to his discussion of the "showy" spiritual gifts.
Simply put, he says, "Pursue love" (1 Corinthians 14:1, NASB).
That two-word expression is a command. He is not talking about
a neat idea or a helpful suggestion for a group of diversely gifted
people. He's telling us what we *must* do. He's saying that we need
to chase after love with the intent of making it our own. That's
what the expression means. Love is necessary, and we must go
after love until we make it our own. The *New Living Translation*
puts it this way: "Let love be your highest goal!"

This command reminds me of the orders given by the line-
backer coach on the sideline of the Pittsburgh Steelers. The
coach circles up his men, looks each one of them in the eye, and

screams, "When we blitz and I assign you the quarterback, you better make sure nothing stops you from getting to him. I don't care what the other team does, you do it one better and put your hands on him. And until you do so, you chase him! You chase him! Hunt him down!" Once all those words penetrate the players' thick helmets, everyone realizes that the coach's orders are not optional. They're not just a nice addition to the defensive scheme. Chasing down the quarterback is the *only way* for the team to succeed.

The same goes for us. We've got to find a way to love. We've got to take the initiative and do whatever it takes to make love happen. And I think you'll agree that when we become last, surrender our rights, and give up our selfish desires, loving suddenly becomes a whole lot easier—it becomes a way of life.

The Response-Ability of Love

Why do we work at loving others? It's not just because God commanded us to love others. It's because love is the only thing that makes sense. For those of us who have a biblically informed relationship with God, love is the fruit of our walk with God. Let me explain what I mean.

You sin. I think you know that. Everyone sins. Your pastor sins. The author of this book sins. We all sin. I don't remind you of that so we can have a big pity party. I say that to remind you and also to reinforce the fact that we are all in dire need of some undeserved backing. The Bible calls it grace. It eliminates the pressure of having to be something we're not—perfect. It stops the pity party before it starts, because the assurance of God's timely support in our broken lives offers constant hope.

Why bring up grace? Because the active nature of your love

is best fueled by the grace and mercy you yourself have received. God doesn't instruct you to love people and then leave you to your own devices. He gives you the ability to love others by loving you first (and always). One of the simplest verses in the Bible is also one of the most profound: "We love, because He first loved us" (1 John 4:19, NASB). This elementary principle is the cornerstone of Christian love.

Love is not merely a warm, fuzzy feeling. It's an *action* based on a *reaction* to God's gracious initiative. Since God gives us room to fail, we can give others room to fail. Since God reaches out to us even when we don't have it all together, we can reach out to others when they're far from perfect. Since God patiently sticks with us no matter what, we can stick with others through thick and thin. Since God looks out for us even when we don't deserve it, we can love others when they don't treat us right. Do you get the point? Our ability to love is directly related to our response to the love Jesus has for us, the extent of which he demonstrated by voluntarily going to the cross to take the punishment we deserve.

Do you know what this means? It means that it's not up to you alone to initiate acts of love. You're not on your own with the burden of mustering up the energy to care. You just have to *respond* to the love of God that's available to you all the time.

Let me tell you how it works for me. When I feel like lashing out at someone who's treated me wrong, I try (though not always successfully) to replay the words Jesus spoke from the cross: "Father, forgive them, for they don't know what they are doing" (Luke 23:34). If he could take those insults and that pain in a grand effort to prove his love for me, then it is only reasonable and right that I respond in kind.

When I truly love others, what I'm doing is remembering the way Christ pursued me and imitating the unconditional love he has for me. The same principle works when I don't feel like doing anything for anyone. I try to think of Jesus' words to his Father as he prayed in the Garden of Gethsemane: "I want your will to be done, not mine" (Matthew 26:39). When I feel that I'm too good to stoop down and help people, I remember how the God of the universe came to earth, took on human flesh, humbled himself, and became obedient even to the point of death. I recall his words, "The Son of Man came not to be served but to serve others and to give his life" (Matthew 20:28). Jesus became last for my sake. And when I look at his face and contemplate his commitment to me, I am left with only one response: love. I am not conjuring up some religious virtue; I am simply letting the reaction to such powerful love do what it does. And I am experiencing what the apostle Paul affirmed when he said, "Christ's love has moved me to such extremes" (2 Corinthians 5:14, *The Message*).

When Gifts Have Downsides, Love Is the Answer

Love for others *is* simply our response to God's love, but because of our sinful nature, we are hardwired in ways that don't make loving easy. For instance, my personality does not naturally exude kindness. You might be able to tell just from reading this book that like the prophets in the Bible, I often (but not always) see life in terms of black and white, right and wrong. Unfortunately, the gift of prophecy (I'm talking about declaring God's truth, not predicting future events) can make me quick to judge and put people in their place. This downside of my gift means that I have to somehow balance the way I'm wired with the *hands-down, without-a-doubt-superior* way of love. I can still use my gift to help weed out sin from the world around me, but I must be careful to do so with kindness and compassion.

What is your gift? Figuring out how God has equipped you to serve him and his people is extremely important. Identifying your gift empowers you to contribute in a deep and satisfying way to God's story, a story that is thousands of years longer than your life span and infinitely bigger than you are. You need to make every effort to figure out how God has designed you. Equally important, you need to spend time in God's Word and prayer to discover the *weaknesses* that come with the way you're wired. As a prophet, I'm quick to call out sin when I see it, but that can push me dangerously close to exuding harshness instead of kindness, arrogance instead of meekness. How are you wired? And what weaknesses—whether you know it or not—are impeding your pursuit of love?

Does your gift of mercy empower you to love the hurting and confused but cause you to shy away from sharing the truth? Could it be that God's clear standards for living get swept under the rug in your effort to make people feel better? Remember that love "does not rejoice about injustice but rejoices whenever the truth wins out" (1 Corinthians 13:6). That's the kind of love we must develop.

Does your intellectual pursuit to understand the Bible help you to teach people the truth but perhaps make you arrogant or self-righteous? Balancing out dangerous by-products is equally as important as explaining the truth. Perhaps your leadership skills can help an organization meet its goals efficiently and achieve success, but it's widely known that you drop people who don't fit into your plans. Remember, "Love never gives up, never loses faith" (1 Corinthians 13:7). Each one of us needs to check and see how the dangers of our strengths must be curbed to make way for our fervent pursuit of love.

Tough Love

Allow me to stop here and get a bit personal, because some of you might be starting to glorify this pursuit of love in ways I don't mean. You might be thinking about how you want to visit a nursing home for an hour and show your kindness, or work with children on Sunday and demonstrate your patience, or mentor someone each week and practice never giving up on them. Although these pursuits are lovely, they tend to be a bit more grandiose than the grassroots type of love I'm talking about. In my opinion, the kind of love that is most difficult to get ahold of—and often most rewarding—involves the people we run across most often in the mundane circumstances of life. Your family, classmates, noisy apartment neighbors, colleagues, and friends all fit this category. Too often we bring our sensitivity and selfless thinking just to special events and not to the people God puts directly in our paths. Too many Christians reflect genuine, heartfelt love at "ministry events," but once they're on the way home or back at work or school, their personalities change completely, and the love is turned off like a faucet. I know I'm susceptible. Are you?

Of all the texts used to describe the key to true love, I believe this one hits the mark true and deep:

> [Love] is not irritable, and it keeps no record of being wronged. 1 CORINTHIANS 13:5

It's easy to love when others love you in return. It's simple to love a person who has a clean track record. But how do you love a person who has treated his wife and children wrongly or has maxed out the charge cards until the family is drowning in debt? How do you remain calm, patient, and loving with those whose history is negative or who have offended you deeply? The key is to refuse to dwell on that history.

Paul brings up this same principle when he describes to a church family in Ephesus what love in action really looks like: "Always be humble and gentle. Be patient with each other, making allowance for each other's faults because of your love" (Ephesians 4:2). Loving people means leaving them a big buffer zone for blowing it. It means that we make room for people's garbage and issues instead of standing ready to condemn. We give those problems and shortfalls a separate room, if you will, because that's what God has done for us.

If we truly want to make an impact for God in our generation, we have to pass on to others what God has given us: unconditional love, love that isn't dependent on a person's actions or performance. Does God stick with us and give us room to blow it time and time again? Yes. He's there 24-7. He never leaves us. He never fails. And neither does love. That is the constant inspiration we need in order to love in the tough, gritty, mundane places of life. And let me tell you, that kind of love is not mundane at all. It's one of the most amazing, rewarding characteristics any of us can develop.

Making Your Gifts . . . Worthless?

Are you hoping to be a bold speaker for God someday? Are you training to become a pastor or missionary? Are you honing your leadership skills or learning how to motivate people to follow God? Maybe you are consistently sharing your faith and finding ways to do that better and better. Perhaps you are working diligently to build your knowledge, gaining wisdom, or praying for miracles. Paul says that all of these things are good, and he even stakes the health and effectiveness of God's church on the ability of people to employ their diverse, God-given gifts. But sometimes what's *good* can be the enemy of what's *best*.

We can make the mistake of chasing after a better opportunity to use our gifts or pursuing some new training to enhance our gifts while forgetting to chase after the *hands-down, without-a-doubt-superior* way of love.

What's the big deal? you ask. Isn't doing one of those things just as good as doing the other? Well, let's look at Paul's take on it.

If I could speak all the languages of earth and of angels, but didn't love others, I would only be a noisy gong or a clanging cymbal. If I had the gift of prophecy, and if I understood all of God's secret plans and possessed all knowledge, and if I had such faith that I could move mountains, but didn't love others, I would be nothing. If I gave everything I have to the poor and even sacrificed my body, I could boast about it; but if I didn't love others, I would have gained nothing.

1 CORINTHIANS 13:1-3

So, what's the verdict on being good with your gifts but lacking love? Paul concludes that without genuine love, even the most miraculous, mind-bending, jaw-dropping, best-selling talents and gifts become no good. They lose all value. A person's gifts are worthless. In that scenario—being good with your gifts, but lacking love—everything you say is ineffective. Everything you know is irrelevant. Everything you believe is insufficient. Everything you give is insignificant. Everything you accomplish is inadequate.

The fact is, *nothing* has any impact if we don't have love.
So I have to ask you, Got love?

Jesus Knows

Although friends and family can help you determine whether
you've "got love," God has an inside track to your heart. He knows
if you are really trying to respond to his love by loving others with
your God-given abilities. He also knows if you're just slapping
Christian labels across your public efforts to please people and
to stroke your own ego. The writer of Proverbs says it this way:

> People may be right in their own eyes, but the LORD examines
> their heart.   PROVERBS 21:2

God examines your heart to see why you do what you do. He's
interested in your motives, in what's driving you. Many of us want
to serve God but can hardly serve the girl next to us. We want
to give our all for God, but we can't give a couple of minutes to
the guy who's hurting. We promise to love God forever, but we
struggle to stay true to our word with family members. It's time to
take John's encouragement seriously:

> Dear children, let's not merely say that we love each other; let
> us show the truth by our actions.   1 JOHN 3:18

Genuine love overflows most when I lay down my own desires and
put others' needs and interests above my own. In other words, I
lay down my life just as Jesus did for me. I'm becoming last so
that someone else can experience a blessing. What can I do to
make my wife's day? How can I bless my children? What small

gift can I pick up for my neighbor to share Christ's love? Why don't I stop and help that woman whose car is stalled on the side of the road?

None of us wants to get to the end of our life and be shocked to realize that we wasted our talents because we forgot the most important thing: love. None of us wants to go through life chasing love, trying to make it our own, only to find that in the end we were just building our own reputations. Our gifts are good, but they must be balanced—even overshadowed—by a love that has legs, a profound love that takes action and thrives even in the mundane places of life.

Do you understand the concept of being last? Have you relinquished your *self*? Are you pursuing love? Think about the past few weeks, and line up your actions with the standards in 1 Corinthians 13:4-8. Perhaps it's time to sit down with God and ask him how you're doing. Seek his unbiased evaluation of your "self" life. What impact is your love having? Are you "others" focused? How is your love measuring up to the plans God has for your life?

Jesus knows your heart, and as you pray and pore over the Scriptures, he can reveal truths to you that will cause your love to rise like the ocean tide and sweep others into his Kingdom!

5

God Can Use . . . Anybody

"Being Last" by Living a Life of Humility

This is what the LORD says: "Heaven is my throne, and the earth

is my footstool. Could you build me a temple as good as that?

Could you build me such a resting place? My hands have made

both heaven and earth; they and everything in them are mine.

I, the LORD, have spoken! I will bless those who have humble

and contrite hearts, who tremble at my word."

———————————— ISAIAH 66:1-2 ————————————

There is something profoundly freeing and supernaturally powerful about acknowledging our sins, our fears, and our shortcomings to God. Throughout the Scriptures we're told that when a person—*any person*—has a "humble and contrite" heart, suddenly God can use that individual in bold and creative new ways to advance his Kingdom. Who is humble and contrite? The one who desires to be last.

Take a moment to think about yourself, your childhood, your family. What kind of relationship did you have with your mom, dad, sisters, brothers? How did you treat one another? Was it a "me first" family environment? What kind of example was set? Would you say you came from a rough home or perhaps a dysfunctional family? Do you have scars from your past that you believe prevent you from doing anything "great" for God?

Many psychologists, truant officers, and even some Christian thinkers will tell you that your childhood years essentially determine what you can and cannot become. They say that the things you experienced within your family—or did not experience because your family disintegrated—determine how you will act for the rest of your life. This line of thinking is called environmental determinism. Instead of saying, "The devil made me do it," environmental determinism says, "My family made me do it!" But the truth is that this is just another in a long line of "justified excuses" that certain "experts" in our society have created to rationalize behavior that was once simply unacceptable.

Certainly it's natural for each of us to pick up character traits from the people around us during our childhood years. Our environment does play a role in our development, but a person's failures and successes, weaknesses and strengths cannot be explained solely on this basis. How much hope is there for the hundreds of thousands of people who've come from messed up families? Can they dare to expect a better life? Or should they simply buckle up for the bumpy ride that is their destiny because of a negative childhood experience?

To answer that, let's take a look at a young man from the Bible named Josiah, who came from just about the roughest background any of us can imagine. The men in his family—far from being good examples to follow—were God haters and scoundrels. Starting with Josiah's grandfather Manasseh, the bar was already set below ground level.

Manasseh removed essentially everything in Judah designed to promote the worship of the one true God. Anything holy that remained he desecrated with unholy and unlawful objects from other religions. In other words, he took God's plan for how to order life in southern Israel and scrapped it for some ideas he'd heard from his Middle Eastern neighbors. Because of the sorcery and witchcraft he practiced, at the height of his reign Manasseh even had one of his own sons burned alive on an altar as a sacrifice to a false god. If that doesn't mess up a family, I don't know what would.

Not surprisingly, Amon followed in his father's footsteps:

> [Amon] did what was evil in the LORD's sight, just as his father, Manasseh, had done. He followed the example of his father, worshiping the same idols his father had worshiped. He abandoned the LORD, the God of his ancestors, and he refused to follow the LORD's ways. 2 KINGS 21:20-22

Amon, Josiah's father, turned out to be such a rotten king that the people who knew him best plotted together and had him assassinated in his own palace. His death served as the exclamation point to his brief and pathetic rule over the land of Judah. But with his pedigree, should anyone have expected anything different? What would become of his offspring? People would naturally expect the same from his children, wouldn't they? Yet God had other plans.

The Third-Grade King

> Josiah was eight years old when he became king, and he reigned in Jerusalem thirty-one years. His mother was Jedidah, the daughter of Adaiah from Bozkath. He did what was pleasing in the LORD's sight and followed the example of his ancestor David. He did not turn away from doing what was right. 2 KINGS 22:1-2

The story of Josiah blows my mind, first because Josiah drew a line in the sand, severing himself from the rotten heritage of his father and grandfather and doing what was right like his ancestor David. So even the youngest people can choose to be last and put God first. But what's doubly shocking is that Josiah was *eight years old* when he became king. That is ridiculous! Today's average eight-year-old is in second or third grade and is just learning how to multiply, divide, and spell. Imagine what it would be like if the United States Constitution were amended so that a third grader could run for president. Although that boy or girl may have some good insights on primary education, how could he or she be expected to devise a plan for balancing the budget or setting foreign policy?

It was about 1980 when I was the age of Josiah when he became king. I was living in Wisconsin at the time and working on growing stronger bones through the intake of excessive amounts of milk, yogurt, and cheese curds (yes, the cheese that squeaks when you chew it). Our public schools encouraged the mass consumption of dairy products, and "milk call" went hand in hand with roll call each morning. When your name was called, you answered with the proverbial "Here" and then followed up with your request for either white or chocolate milk, which you would then receive during various milk breaks throughout the day.

One day, having noticed that my friend Mary Ellen was absent, I began to develop a clever scheme that I thought would result in more chocolate milk for me. When the teacher called Mary Ellen's name during roll call, I would simply impersonate her and request another chocolate milk. Okay, you may not think the plan was so clever, but for me, an eight-year-old at the time, it was genius, pure genius!

So I sat and waited as each student's name was called and each one made the usual milk request (white milk for those with stricter parents, and chocolate for those with more accommodating moms or dads). Soon Mary Ellen's name was called. In my best prepubescent voice I answered, "Here . . . chocolate." I quickly scanned my classmates and with a lowered brow, placed my index finger over my mouth in perpendicular fashion—the universal sign for "Don't tell, or you'll get it."

Unfortunately, even with my natural high voice and commanding influence over my peers, I had failed to realize that my teacher did an eye check with each call. I was caught! My ploy had flopped, and after getting a good laugh from the class and a stern warning from my teacher, I was forced to nurse the usual one carton of chocolate milk with my lunch.

Think about the tunnel vision I had at Josiah's age. My greatest plans were aimed at obtaining more chocolate milk, and I couldn't even do that successfully. Compare that with the responsibilities Josiah had at age eight. Imagine the baggage he was forced to carry: His father had recently been assassinated, his uncle had been burned alive in a pagan sacrifice, and his grandfather was a notorious God hater and idol worshiper. And here was Josiah, the young man in the family, becoming king over Judah!

Meltdown

Although the Bible doesn't go into detail about the first eighteen years of Josiah's reign, it does tell us that when he was twenty-six, something happened that would alter the course of his life and the lives of many under his rule.

When it came time to collect the Temple tax so that carpenters, builders, and masons could be hired and wood and stone purchased for repairs, Josiah assigned Shaphan, his CFO, to collect the money from the high priest, Hilkiah. Hilkiah gave Shaphan the money and also an old scroll that had recently been found:

> Hilkiah the high priest said to Shaphan the court secretary, "I have found the Book of the Law in the LORD's Temple!" Then Hilkiah gave the scroll to Shaphan, and he read it. Shaphan went to the king and reported, "Your officials have turned over the money collected at the Temple of the LORD to the workers and supervisors at the Temple." Shaphan also told the king, "Hilkiah the priest has given me a scroll." So Shaphan read it to the king. When the king heard what was written in the Book of the Law, he tore his clothes in despair. Then he gave these orders to Hilkiah the priest, Ahikam son of Shaphan, Acbor son of Micaiah, Shaphan the court secretary, and Asaiah the king's personal adviser: "Go to the Temple and speak to the LORD for me and for the people and for all Judah. Inquire about the words written in this scroll that has been found. For the LORD's great anger is burning against us because our ancestors have not obeyed the words in this scroll. We have not been doing everything it says we must do."
>
> 2 KINGS 22:8-13

Taking Responsibility

Have you ever been around people who constantly push problems off themselves and onto others? When you zoom in on Josiah's words, you might get the impression that he is one of those people: "The LORD's great anger is burning against us because *our ancestors* have not obeyed the words in this scroll" (emphasis added). His statement sounds like the classic depersonalization response I often encounter at different speaking events around the world. People often thank me for a message that "my friend John," or "my son Brian," or "my mother" desperately needed to hear. Those kinds of comments can be the most discouraging ones I hear, because they only affirm how much the person talking to me failed to be *personally* affected by the message.

Is that how Josiah responded to the words written in the Book of the Law? Not at all. Josiah did not skirt the issue or his own responsibility. He did not merely point the finger of blame at his wretched ancestors. No, his first words to his advisors were, "Go to the Temple and speak to the LORD *for me* and for the people and for all Judah." And note his last words: "*We* have not been doing everything [this scroll] says *we* must do" (emphases added). Josiah humbly yet boldly placed himself at the front of the line of those needing to do business with God. He acknowledged that he was partly responsible for the Lord's anger. His last words show that he associated himself with everyone else who had not been doing what the scroll said. When he heard the words of the Lord, he tore his clothing in despair and admitted, "We've got a problem. It's our fault!" No dodging the blame. No passing the buck. He owned up to his own faults and the mistakes of others. Then he asked what he could do to make things right.

Josiah wasn't afraid to admit his mistakes. As king, he could blame the priests or his advisors. But instead, he was willing to place himself on an equal footing with his subjects, to share the responsibility for failing to read and obey what the scroll said.

He wasn't afraid to be last. He simply wanted to please God, no matter what other people thought of him.

What a way to live.

God Loves to Hear "I'm Sorry"

When Josiah instructed his advisors to ask the Lord what to do in their sinful situation, the five advisors went to talk to a prophet, a godly woman named Huldah, who had a tremendous ability to discern God's intentions. After hearing the advisors' inquiry, she confirmed that God's anger was indeed burning against Judah and would result in punishment. However, Josiah's brokenness over his lack of leadership and the sin of his people had touched the gracious heart of God and had turned his wrath away from Josiah's generation. Huldah instructed the men to give Josiah this message:

> You were sorry and humbled yourself before the LORD when you heard what I said against this city and its people—that this land would be cursed and become desolate. You tore your clothing in despair and wept before me in repentance. And I have indeed heard you, says the LORD.   2 KINGS 22:19

God loves to hear someone offer a genuine "I'm sorry, Father. Please forgive me." He loves a broken heart. Like a parent, he relishes it when his children repent and show a strong desire to please him. In both the Old and New Testaments we find the idea that God gives grace to the humble but opposes the proud (see Psalm 138:6; James 4:6; 1 Peter 5:5).

God's heart bleeds compassion when it sees true humility. When the Father finds you weeping because of your sin or falling on your knees at the realization of how your unrighteousness has offended him, he instantly reaches out with arms of forgiveness. It doesn't happen only when he is in a certain mood or when he hears specific words. It happens anytime you become truly aware of the reality and magnitude of your sin and your heart spells out in a language that only God can read, "I'm sorry. I'm so sorry, and I want to change." Josiah's heart spelled out those words, and God forgave him. And from then on, Josiah became one of the few men of his time of whom it was said, "He did what was pleasing in the LORD's sight and followed the example of his ancestor David. He did not turn away from doing what was right" (2 Kings 22:2).

Little Guys Can Make a Big Difference

We can learn a lot from a young guy like Josiah, who started out with the cards stacked against him but became one of the greatest kings in all the Bible. We can also learn a lot from a dry goods and drapery salesman named Ed Kimball, who lived in Boston. No kidding. It may not sound intriguing, but you'll dig it, I promise. Just keep reading.

In the midst of his big-time career, Ed Kimball volunteered to teach Sunday school to a group of junior-high boys. Every Sunday he saw the same young men, built stronger and stronger relationships with them, and taught them about Jesus. Ed was no famous evangelist, but he was doing his part. Soon after starting his junior-high ministry, Ed decided to visit one of his students at the shoe store owned by the boy's uncle. It was April 17, 1856. He dropped by the store, introduced himself to the uncle, and asked where Dwight was. Dwight's uncle directed Ed to the back room, where Ed proceeded to sit down and have an in-depth conversation with Dwight.

Ed cut to the chase pretty quickly. Because he had seen Dwight on Sundays for a while, he told him that he thought it was time the boy considered becoming a Christian. Later, Dwight said that the look in Ed's eyes during that conversation broke his heart and moved him to a complete commitment to Christ. Dwight's last name was Moody—yes, the same Dwight L. Moody who spoke to tens of millions of people during his ministry and may have led one million to Christ in his lifetime.

Are you listening for God's promptings? Are you making the time to respond in quiet obedience? Apparently Ed Kimball was, when God nudged him to visit Dwight Moody at the shoe store. And look how many lives Moody touched because Ed Kimball was obedient. Not only that, at one of Moody's meetings in Chicago, he counseled a man named J. Wilbur Chapman and helped him become certain of his salvation. Chapman spent some time working for Billy Sunday, the former baseball player who met Christ at a meeting led by the Pacific Garden Mission and became a fiery evangelist.

During Billy Sunday's ministry, he eventually traveled to Charlotte, North Carolina, where he held a number of evangelistic meetings. Out of these meetings grew what eventually became the Charlotte Businessmen's Club, which played a role in inviting Mordecai Ham to hold meetings in Charlotte in 1934. During one of those meetings, a Christian farmer in the audience was trying to figure out how to evangelize his young neighbor, when he got an idea. He went to his neighbor's house and asked the sixteen-year-old boy, William, if he would drive him to the meetings. Of course, if you're a sixteen-year-old boy and someone asks you to drive him anywhere, you'll go! So, William drove his farmer friend to the meetings, and sure enough, several nights later, William met Jesus.

You might recognize William by his more familiar name, Billy. That's right, Billy Graham became a Christian through the ministry of Mordecai Ham and just a few years later became an evangelist himself. Since that seed was watered, Billy Graham has presented the gospel to nearly one billion people worldwide via live speaking engagements and satellite broadcasts.

But this remarkable chain of events doesn't stop with Billy Graham. In 1957 Billy Graham spoke at Madison Square Garden, where Randy, a thirteen-year-old boy, was in attendance. After hearing the message, Randy realized that it was time to commit his life to Christ, so he made his way to the front of the famed Garden and prayed. Years later, Randy became a pastor and had three boys of his own. One day one of Randy's sons asked him, "Dad, why don't you let me take Communion?"

With a serious but inviting tone, Randy replied, "Jeremy, it's because you're not a Christian yet."

Randy Kingsley is my dad. About a year later he helped me to pray and ask Jesus to be my Savior and the Lord of my life. The chain is unbroken, and I can't tell you how thankful I am for Ed Kimball, the drapery salesman. I imagine Ed may have struggled with how much he could do as a salesman who taught Sunday school to junior-high boys, but God had big plans. Ed's legacy has touched the lives of billions of people and changed my own life almost 150 years later. I can't wait to find him in heaven and thank him.

Ed Kimball's life had an impact on Dwight Moody, whose counsel helped to transform J. Wilbur Chapman, whose life touched the life of Billy Sunday, whose ministry affected Mordecai Ham, whose teaching reached the soul of Billy Graham, whose boldness pierced the heart of my father, whose guidance led me to Christ.

And now it's your turn.

Why Are You Here?

Whose life will be radically impacted by your existence? I can almost guarantee that if you become last, develop a humble and contrite heart, and tremble at God's Word, he will most certainly use you beyond your dreams or expectations.

Trust me when I say that God can use anybody—a farmer with an idea, a drapery salesman who teaches Sunday school, an eight-year-old king—and you. It doesn't matter what kind of personal sin you've committed, what kind of family baggage you carry, or how much—or how little—money you've got in the bank. You don't have to speak with an intriguing accent or be some charismatic star. You don't even have to be all that smart. I'm living proof—I didn't get a single A in four years of college. God simply takes meek people who are available and empowers them to change the world. So, if you want to be used, God is ready and willing to make you able.

In my ministry I travel throughout the year, and that means leaving my sweet little family behind for short periods of time. Although my wife and I are totally on board with God's plan and purpose for our ministry, I face a different challenge when it comes to our young children. One of the best ways I can get across to them that they should be happy and excited about my trips is to let them know that God is attempting to use me when I travel. To make that message clear, I began the tradition of sitting my son Jaden down before each trip and explaining that I am going on a trip to tell people about Jesus. With my luggage sitting nearby, I tell him that Daddy's desire is to help people to know and love Jesus. Then, with a kiss and a prayer, I head out the door.

When Jaden turned three, I was glad to see that the tradition was having an effect. One day he came trudging out of our master bedroom, dragging my suitcase behind him with a determined look in his eyes. As he struggled to move the bag, which could have housed him and a friend, we asked him what he intended to do. He replied boldly, "I tell people Jesus!" One part of me smiled, and another part wept, because although his imitation struck me as syrupy cute, it also struck me that this could be the foundation of a life that God uses to change the world. I can only hope and pray that his desire grows and becomes a daily intention that's nurtured in prayer and lived out in his actions.

Of course, you may come to the conclusion that being used by God is optional rather than imperative. You may think that God will figure out a way to accomplish his purposes even if you don't step up and offer your life. The fact is, God can certainly perform amazing miracles without you, but statistically speaking, the Bible tells us that his favorite way to reach people is through other people.

He can use other things, but he loves to use people. That means that he wants to use *you* to bring smiles to the hurting. You are a bearer of his message of salvation to the lost. Every one of us is just the right person for the job—if we want to be. My dad once told me, "If you love Jesus and ask him to use you, watch out!" His advice gave me the boldness to lead a friend to Jesus when I was in fifth grade; it's probably why I still have boldness today.

Do you want to be used by God? If you need a place to start, try praying this simple prayer each day: "God, please wash away my sins and make me meek. Help me to have a humble, contrite heart. I volunteer to be last—for your sake. Will you please use me and give me the desire to be used?"

If you are ready to change when God shows you your sin, and

you are consistently praying this prayer, then *watch out!* God just may make you the next Josiah who changes a nation, or the next Ed Kimball whose faithful obedience changes a generation. You might even help change the world!

6

The Rebel

"Being Last" by Living a Life of Submission

Do you know any rebels? You know, people who think their mission in life is to go against anything and everything? Even if they have no problem with what is going on, they cannot stop themselves from finding something to disagree with and jumping over to the other side of the line. When you talk about how great Ohio State football is, they start talking up the Michigan Wolverines. When you decide it's time to exercise, they decide it's time for a nap. If you say you love Coca-Cola, they feel the need to bring up Pepsi. They just refuse to buy into anyone else's ideas. It's all about their opinion and their way!

You probably know these kinds of people. You may even be one of them. Maybe you're the one who rebels against parents, teachers, bosses, the government, or even Jesus himself. So let's think about what fuels a rebellious spirit. Why do people rebel against even the inconsequential preferences of their friends? And more important, why do they rebel against God's mandates for their lives? Why is it always "me first" with rebellious people? I propose that rebellion does not thrive alone. Just as a fungus needs dark, damp areas to grow, rebellion requires the breeding ground of a proud human heart. Rebellion and pride are best "buds."

On the other side of the road stands submission. Submission works in the opposite direction of rebellion. When rebellion says, "I couldn't care less what you want," submission says, "Not my will but yours be done." When rebellion says, "I've got better plans," submission says, "I trust your ideas more than my own." Where rebellion just can't wait to show how wrong you are, submission recognizes that you're right.

Submission is a staple of being last. Does that sound like Jesus and how he related to the Father? Submission works in partnership with a friend quite different from the way rebellion's *pride* does. Submission's lifelong friend is *humility*. Before you are ready to promote the cause of others and, in particular, the cause of God, you have to recognize that you are not "all that." The story of Jonah is a prime example.

The Wickedness of Nineveh

The LORD gave this message to Jonah son of Amittai: "Get up and go to the great city of Nineveh. Announce my judgment against it because I have seen how wicked its people are."

JONAH 1:1-2

As the book opens, God tells Jonah to go to a city called Nineveh and announce judgment because of the people's wickedness. That raises this question: Just how wicked were the Ninevites?

The Old Testament prophet Nahum called Nineveh "the city of murder and lies" (Nahum 3:1)—not the sort of description you'd put on a travel poster promoting tourism: "Come to Nineveh, where everyone lies and dies!" In fact, most people in the surrounding region were not attracted to the luxuries of Nineveh; they were afraid of her immense power and brutality. Nineveh was not some hole-in-the-wall town. It was the capital city of Assyria, one of the great empires in the Middle East. In Jonah's time, the population in the greater metropolitan area probably approached 200,000, and those 200,000 people were part of an empire that ruled a portion of the world because of its cruelty toward its enemies.

When the Assyrians wanted to expand their territory through conquest, they did not practice the dictates of the Geneva Convention—they were a few millennia before its time. According to some records, they gathered their prisoners (such as the Jews in northern Palestine), cut off a few heads, and drained the blood into buckets. Then they dipped branches into the blood and painted graffiti all around the city. Imagine—no respect, no boundaries, no sense of decency, no regard for the inherent value God placed on human life.

So when God said of Nineveh, "I have seen how wicked its people are," he was not talking about improper attitudes behind their religious devotion or about their selfishness in not saving the last piece of pie for Mom. He was not charged up over a few accidental errors or unintentional sins. He was fuming at an empire that had been built on bloodshed, violence, torture, and disgrace. The Assyrians killed and deceived their neighbors and stood condemned on numerous counts before the God who had given them life. So God was going to act against them, as has been his policy since he described it to Noah (see Genesis 9:6). The Assyrians had taken people's lives, and therefore, others would take their lives. Yet God in his inexplicable blend of justice *and* mercy picked out Jonah to go and warn the Ninevites of the coming catastrophe. God does punish wickedness, but he also forgives the sins and redirects the lives of those who recognize their wrongs. So at the beginning of Jonah's story, he gets to be the guy who gives the Ninevites one last chance.

Jonah's Rebellion

How does Jonah respond to this once-in-a-lifetime opportunity? "Jonah got up and went in the opposite direction to get away from the LORD. He went down to the port of Joppa, where he found a ship leaving for Tarshish. He bought a ticket and went on board, hoping to escape from the LORD by sailing to Tarshish" (Jonah 1:3).

The passage is somewhat shocking when we consider the details. Of course, it's obvious that Jonah didn't do what he was told. That much is clear. But his refusal does not end just with a big "NO!" to God and a return to his everyday life. Jonah doesn't ignore God's command because he's preoccupied or lazy or even unclear about what to do. His refusal is flat-out rebellion, where God's directions to go four or five hundred miles northeast turn into a plan to go twelve hundred miles west. The names *Tarshish* and *Nineveh* do not sound alike. Jonah did not misunderstand what God said. He didn't have a bad sense of direction because he was unable to follow a MapQuest printout. No, he faced off with God, said no, and then hightailed it out of Dodge. That's rebellion. That is "me first" to the max.

Now before we go any further, I need to point out that there is a difference between rebellion and struggle. I used to struggle with having to mow the lawn when my father told me to. I dreaded that "let's talk about your next chore" tone. Finding me relaxing somewhere in the house, Dad would look me straight in the eye until he had pierced my youthful soul. Then, with two simple words—"It's time"—he would designate the next afternoon as chore time.

Something would sink in my soul. I felt as if tomorrow were now a waste and that *I* should be able to determine what I did or did not do. I would begin to protest, "But, Dad!"—until a glimpse of his eyes and recollections of a hundred other such conversations put me back in my place. "All right," I'd say.

What if I didn't struggle, though? What if I just flat out rebelled against my father's wishes and, like Jonah, went in the opposite direction? What if the next time my dad asked me to mow the lawn, I said no and then proceeded to haul the mower and gas can to the middle of the yard, spray five gallons of gas, toss a lighted match, and surprise Dad with a field of flames and an exploding mower? I'd be a dead man.

But that kind of scenario is exactly what Jonah did to God. He not only said no but also took steps that would make it impossible to obey God's command. It was no and then some!

What Does It Take to Break You?

What happened when Jonah set out to escape from the Lord?

> The LORD hurled a powerful wind over the sea, causing a violent storm that threatened to break the ship apart. Fearing for their lives, the desperate sailors shouted to their gods for help and threw the cargo overboard to lighten the ship. But all this time Jonah was sound asleep down in the hold. So the captain went down after him. "How can you sleep at a time like this?" he shouted. "Get up and pray to your god! Maybe he will pay attention to us and spare our lives." JONAH 1:4-6

At first glance, these verses just seem to be pushing the plot forward with some information about the nameless sailors' reaction to the squall they encountered on the Mediterranean Sea. They got scared, threw some cargo overboard, and started calling to their gods for help. But we shouldn't brush aside this passage too easily, because the impact heightens when you consider that the original audience of this prophetic narrative would have been Israelites. Jonah's story was recorded for their instruction. So how would they have reacted to the sailors' actions?

Well, first, they would have scoffed at the pathetic attempts of the sailors to compensate for the destructive storm by lightening the load or by praying to pagan gods. No human maneuvers or nonexistent pagan deities could have thwarted what the God of Israel was orchestrating from heaven. Second, they would have been offended by Jonah's inaction. The pagan captain is the one to tell Jonah to wake up and pray, instead of the other way around, and when the captain gives his reasoning, he mentions that "maybe" Jonah's God will be concerned about them and help. A good Jew of the time would have known that God does rescue those who call to him *humbly*. So they would likely have been offended by the lack of power attributed to their God. This perspective of the original audience illuminates the literary impact of the story so far: A calamity can be an act of the one true God who intends to use it to teach the recipients a lesson.

Had Jonah learned his lesson? Not yet. Even at the request (and subtle rebuke) of the captain, Jonah tried to hide from God's corrective calamity. But the crew had an ancient practice designed to identify the guilty man among them:

The crew cast lots to see which of them had offended the gods and caused the terrible storm. When they did this, the lots identified Jonah as the culprit. "Why has this awful storm come down on us?" they demanded. "Who are you? What is your line of work? What country are you from? What is your nationality?" JONAH 1:7-8

Jonah's guilt had been revealed. Using an old sailing superstition, God let the whole crew in on the real problem—a foreign passenger had angered a foreign god. At this point Jonah's stiff-necked rebellion started to crumble. He began to realize that his flagrant violation of God's command was going to kill him as well as those around him and that maybe following his own will was not the best idea. Maybe he should have let God's opinion and plan, not his own, be first. So he fessed up:

"I am a Hebrew, and I worship the LORD, the God of heaven, who made the sea and the land." The sailors were terrified when they heard this, for he had already told them he was running away from the LORD. "Oh, why did you do it?" they groaned. And since the storm was getting worse all the time, they asked him, "What should we do to you to stop this storm?" "Throw me into the sea," Jonah said, "and it will become calm again. I know that this terrible storm is all my fault." JONAH 1:9-12

Jonah's confession of rebellion was a long time coming. First, he made a conscious decision to take himself out of God's reach. Then, he had to withstand the subtle insults against his God, whom the sailors had placed among the myriads of pagan gods.

Last, he had to be pegged as the one whose offense had brought on the terrible storm.

What does it take for you? Have you found ways to shrug off your direct refusal to follow God's commands? Have you jumped on the bandwagon of pluralism and sat quietly as your friends and society relegated the one true God to the position of just one option among others of questionable strength? Have you felt yourself becoming the cause of degenerate situations instead of the carrier of blessings to others? Does life always have to revolve around you? God will do whatever it takes to get your attention. Remember, God will even use calamity to teach you a lesson, because the stakes are high for those who refuse him. His discipline is actually an expression of his love.

Is Sin a Private or a Public Matter?

The sailors rowed even harder to get the ship to the land. But the stormy sea was too violent for them, and they couldn't make it. Then they cried out to the LORD, Jonah's God. "O LORD," they pleaded, "don't make us die for this man's sin. And don't hold us responsible for his death. O LORD, you have sent this storm upon him for your own good reasons."

JONAH 1:13-14

Notice that even after the sailors heard Jonah's confession, they still wanted to give him one last chance before following his instructions to toss him overboard to his death. Interestingly, the narrative actually portrays the pagan sailors as the merciful ones, who went to the greatest lengths to preserve Jonah's life while at the same time preserving their own. But of course, their tactics did not succeed, and it came time to throw Jonah overboard. So the sailors prayed for mercy because they did not want their lives to be destroyed as a result of "this man's sin."

These words—"this man's sin"—point out a dangerous reality about sin. As Jonah flees from God's commands on a ship destined for Tarshish, he involves other people in his sin. His rebellion is no private matter. It actually endangers the life of every man with him.

The same is true for us. Not only does our sin introduce destructive consequences into our own lives, but it also introduces those consequences into the lives of those around us. Even if your sin is not public knowledge, it still has public effects. My friend's dad was killed by a drunk driver. Is it a sin to get drunk? Yes. So the sin of one man caused the death of another. This kind of cause-and-effect reality attached to every sin happens all the time, even though more often on a subtle level. Insults destroy people's self-perceptions. Pornography destroys people's marriages. Stealing destroys businesses. Complaining or criticizing ruins the mood in homes and offices. Lying hurts your friends and family. These are the facts. That is one reason why *being last* is so huge. We must learn to consistently put God and others first. Every supposedly "personal" sin you commit affects your public life and the lives of the people who come in contact with you—believe it! You can either be a life-giving agent of God or a human virus infecting every home, office, church, or business you enter.

Out of the Boat and into the Fish

After Jonah's shipmates had prayed for God's mercy, "the sailors were awestruck by the LORD's great power, and they offered him a sacrifice and vowed to serve him" (Jonah 1:16). That scene would have been unbelievable, wouldn't it? The sailors are fighting for their lives; they pull the old "Red Rover, Red Rover, let's send Jonah over," and the next minute all is well. They are so impressed that they give homage to the God who had just saved them. All of a sudden *they* are putting God first. Now if only Jonah had had that attitude of reverence for God from the beginning, they would not have had to lose all their cargo and escape by the skin of their teeth.

If I had been one of the sailors and had really been concerned about Jonah, my next thought might have been to toss him a rope or a floating box or something to save him. The sailors might even have intended to do that very thing. But Jonah was not around long enough for a normal rescue, because "the LORD had arranged for a great fish to swallow Jonah. And Jonah was inside the fish for three days and three nights" (Jonah 1:17).

I've wondered what life was like for Jonah during his stay in the fish's stomach. If you have ever caught a fish and cleaned it yourself rather than freaked out and made someone else touch the slime and scales, then you have just a bit of personal experience to connect you to Jonah's situation.

There should be a special word to describe the stench that migrates from the fish to your hands. Even if you are able to avoid spreading the odor, removing it from your hands requires a deadly concoction of Irish Spring, vinegar, WD-40, and sandpaper. So can you imagine being in the *stomach* of a fish?

We Do *Not* Serve a God of Second Chances

When Jonah recounts the events in a poetic prayer, he lets us know about his reaction to the fishy experience: "As my life was slipping away, I remembered the LORD. And my earnest prayer went out to you in your holy Temple" (Jonah 2:7). Jonah's rebellion had not left him high and dry; it had left him deep and wet. As Jonah faced the prospect of dying in the fish, he turned to God to see if help could still be found, even after he had refused to repent for so long. He was not disappointed.

Aren't you glad God is *not* a God of second chances? I have heard from others that he is, but the Bible tells a different story. He doesn't give just second chances. With God, *you get way more than two!* We need every one of them, don't we? Of the many characteristics that draw out my admiration for God, his readiness to give more than just a second chance is up there on the list. Our God abounds in love, grace, and mercy. He knows we are weak and fickle, and he gives us room to err and then repent, even if we've done it many times before. We don't find that kind of grace, that forgiving loyalty, too often among human beings. We tend to drop people after one or two mistakes that hurt us, but God stays committed to his creation.

In Jonah's case, God did respond to Jonah's prayer for mercy. However, Jonah's path of restoration was not pretty. I hope he took a bath before he got to Nineveh! In any case, Jonah made it back to land and decided to obey God's command to travel to Nineveh and deliver a message of judgment.

Get Your Hate On

Jonah's task in Nineveh should have elicited a good deal of fleshly pleasure for him. Being an Israelite, Jonah would have hated the Assyrians, who were essentially a terrorist regime polluting the region with their brutal tactics and thirst for power. To announce their imminent destruction should have been a welcome task for Jonah, because everyone loves to see the downfall of those they hate. However, later in the book of Jonah we learn that the prophet's refusal to bring God's message of judgment to Nineveh was motivated by his fear that they would repent and escape destruction (see 4:1-3). The hatred of a proud heart is not easily quelled.

Do you hate anyone? Let me define what I mean. Hate is an emotion fueled by anger, strong dislike, and ill will, often over some conflict with someone or something. Maybe someone insulted you, overlooked you, harmed you, or left you. Maybe you hate a whole group of people and therefore anyone associated with that group, government, or institution. Are you a racist? Are you the CEO of prejudice? Are you the epitome of "me first"? If so, you are familiar with the feeling of loathing you get when you think about the object or objects of your hatred and the hope you have for their demise. Jesus himself speaks of hate as a precursor to murder. It is serious business and a telltale sign of a proud heart.

But the Bible actually encourages one brand of hate. God wants you to get your hate on and drink some God-approved anger until you're brimming with disdain. Romans 12:9 commands it: "Hate what is wrong." The verse is simple. When you see the things that God stands against, you are supposed to hate those things as well. If you see some half-exposed woman on television, you should change the channel in anger that such junk is broadcast so that the whole nation can be moved to lust. If you hear rumors being spread behind someone else's back, it should make you want to kill that conversation and put an end to the gossip. When someone lightly dismisses the significance of Jesus, you should get fired up inside and take an appropriate action so that Jesus gets the respect he deserves. That's the kind of hate that a Christian should know, because that is fueled by biblically recommended, righteous anger.

"Face Pusher" and Forgiveness

I remember hating someone when I was in high school. I was a basketball player first and foremost, but one year my friends and a coach convinced me to join the soccer team. So I went to try-outs and made the team as a backup goalie. With the talent that the guys on the team had, I expected to be on a winning team and enjoy the majority of the games from the bench. Since I really loved basketball, I didn't much mind the arrangement. Unfortunately, our number one goalkeeper failed to block a shot in a preseason game, and in his frustration, he punched the goalpost so hard that he hurt his hand and had to come out of the game. So I went in with the instructions to hit only the ball—not the post. A few days later we learned that the goalie had fractured his wrist and would miss the rest of the season.

Working on a steep learning curve, I quickly began to get a feel for the position, and I didn't do too badly. Between my efforts as goalie and a strong defense in front of me, we were able to work our way into the top ten teams in Prince George County (in southern Washington, D.C.). It was no small accomplishment, considering the competition we faced.

Eventually, we had to face one of the other top-ten teams. In one of the most memorable games, I remember blocking a hard-hit shot and jumping up to punt the ball back down the field to my players. However, the opposing forward whose shot I had just blocked did not stop running at me after I jumped up and began directing my teammates. In fact, he ran right up to me with an open hand and pushed me in the face. No joke. He pushed my face! Then he took off running back down the field, and I couldn't do a thing. I had the ball and needed to punt it from inside the box. So I shook it off and continued to play, fueled by a newfound hatred for an unnamed player on the other team. Let's call him "Face Pusher."

We played the rest of the game scoreless until the last two minutes, when the coach instructed the defense to push up the field. If you're on offense, you love it when your defense pushes up because it gives you more support and a better chance to move the ball down the field for a score. But if you're a goal-keeper, there is nothing exciting about your teammates pushing up and leaving you alone. All it does is leave a huge open field for the other team to break into and run down for an open shot. And of course, that is exactly what happened in the game.

The coach told the defense to push up. I told the defense to stay back. The opposing team kicked the long ball over the defense, and the first one to the ball was their right wing. As he came cruising down the field, I saw there was no way my defense was going to make it back in time. As the player got about thirty yards out, I ran out to cut off his angle, and he then attempted a cross pass to—guess who? That's right, Face Pusher! I cut back to try to block the pass and slid on the ground to ensure that I caught the ball. Unfortunately, our field had some sizeable mounds, divots, and dry spots, so the ball suddenly popped up, I fumbled it, it rolled past me and landed in front of Face Pusher, who trapped the ball, dropped a couple of curse words at me, and with a wide-open net, scored the winning goal.

That play happened twenty years ago, and it still makes me mad. I remember how I treated that guy after the game. You want to talk about being first instead of last. I was a Christian at the time and should have been setting the example, but I was not gonna give that guy a handshake, a "good game"—not a thing! God was giving me a chance to put him first by putting another person ahead of my own personal issues and to show how cool Jesus is, but I said no! I decided that my hatred for Face Pusher was more significant than God's love for him. So I got into my 1982 Bonneville and drove home. If that guy's bus had crashed in front of me and old Face Pusher had been bleeding and crying for help on the side of the road, I couldn't have cared less. Not that day! He had ticked me off, and I hated him. Call me a rebel. Call me proud. I didn't care. It was me first.

Could You Please Get off My Horse?

Later that year, I found myself at a Christian conference, sitting in the back of an auditorium about to listen to a Christian solo artist, but before he got to the second note, I broke into tears. I don't know what magical key he had or what unclassified note he used to open the song, but out of the blue I started losing it. I didn't know why. I was just sitting there and all of a sudden the floodgates opened. I quickly started to wipe my eyes, hoping no one was watching, and thought, *What in the world is going on here?* I wanted it to stop.

Then I began to follow that emotion into a picture that my mind was creating. I saw the entire crowd walking in a big, open field. Teachers, students, young and older people were all walking. In the middle of the field I noticed a big horse, and on that horse sat someone I knew very well—me. Everyone else had to walk, but I got to ride the horse.

Then I noticed Jesus. He was working his way through the crowd toward me. He was touching other people and talking to them, but he was definitely on a mission to have a word with me. When he finally reached me, he said, "Jeremy, I was wondering if you could please get off my horse. I'm the only one who rides up there, and you are a prideful person for taking that seat. So I was wondering if you could please get off my horse." That mental image only made me cry harder. Jesus was pointing out my pride. I was all about being first. I had become a rebellious jerk, and I knew it.

I fell on my knees, face to the floor in that auditorium, and began to pour out my rebellious heart to God: "I'm so sorry. I never want to ride your horse again. For a long time I have secretly thought that I'm better than other people and deserve some sort of special privilege, but I'm sorry. I'm sorry that I even thought I could sit in your place. Forgive me. Please forgive me." I stayed on that auditorium floor for a long time.

As I indicated in the beginning of this chapter, *pride is the partner in the crime of rebellion, but humility is submission's accomplice.* What kind of friends do you keep close to your heart? Being last is all about humility. Do you need to end this chapter with the facedown prayer of an exposed rebel, or are you going to wait for God to get your attention through the wreckage of some extreme measure? This is an issue of pride. Jonah thought he had better travel plans than God, so he set out in the opposite direction from God's revealed path for him.

You have a similar choice. God has laid out his plans for you in the Bible, and you have to decide who gets to sit on the horse and lead the way: you or Jesus. If you want to be first and take control, please reconsider. If you have been on the path of rebellion and can smell the stench stirred up by your sin, it's time to face up to God. You might start facedown with a proud heart, but don't forget to look up and see the face of a forgiving God looking back at you.

Now here's what is interesting: When Jonah went to Nineveh and preached his eight-word message, all the people—from the king to the poorest person—repented! It was the biggest revival in the history of the Old Testament, and God used the formerly rebellious, me-first jerk to bring it about.

Not long ago I was looking in a mirror, and tears began filling my eyes, just like back at that event in high school. I thought about riding on Jesus' horse and about other failures in my life, and I asked God, "After all I've done wrong, all the times I have hurt you, why do you let me travel around the country and teach the Bible to all these people? You know all my sin and all the things in the past that I am ashamed of. Why do I still get the honor of teaching people?"

Here's what he spoke to my heart: *"Because with me, you get way more than two chances!"*

7

Aliens

"Being Last" by Living Life as an Alien

Here's a straightforward question for you: Do you look more like Jesus or more like "the world"? We know that Satan and the world have devised many ways to get us off track, to get us to live a "me first" life. But God's plan is for us to look like Jesus. Throughout his Epistles, the apostle Paul pushes us to a life of imitation. Here's a sampling of what I mean:

> Don't copy the behavior and customs of this world, but let God transform you into a new person by changing the way you think. ROMANS 12:2

> You should imitate me, just as I imitate Christ.
> 1 CORINTHIANS 11:1

> Imitate God . . . in everything you do, because you are his dear children. EPHESIANS 5:1

The Greek word for imitation here is *mimtai*. It's the ancient root word from which we get such English words as *mime* and *mimic.* That connection helps us better understand that Jesus wants our actions to look like his. Look at the example he set. He was humble in birth, in life, and even in death. When we have a question—*any question*—about how to live our lives, we should look first at how he operated while he was on earth and discern the values and character traits that drove him. Then we should mimic what we find.

Are You a Foreigner?

Let's take a few minutes to look at how you compare with the world. Listen to what Peter says about the way Christians should live among unbelievers:

> Dear friends, I warn you as "temporary residents and foreigners" to keep away from worldly desires that wage war against your very souls. Be careful to live properly among your unbelieving neighbors. Then even if they accuse you of doing wrong, they will see your honorable behavior, and they will give honor to God when he judges the world.
>
> 1 PETER 2:11-12

When it comes to how our actions match up to those of the world, we should look different, with a capital *D*. We should look like Jesus. Does that sound weird? Well, maybe weird is the way we're supposed to look sometimes.

Seriously, though, notice the importance this passage places on our actions. When it comes to being a friend of God and an alien in this world, the determining factor is our behavior. Don't overlook that. Too often American churches place so much emphasis on grace and love that we tend to drift away from the nuts and bolts of daily obedience to Christ in our actions.

Do you ever feel as if sometimes the church lacks balance? Back in the 1950s and 1960s, legalism and discipline ran rampant in churches. If you got pregnant out of wedlock, you may have been kicked out of the church and asked not to come back. If you got hooked on cocaine or started going to those new rock-and-roll concerts, you'd better stay away, because there was no place for "your kind of person" in the house of God. The reality of accountability for sin—which is good—was so overemphasized that it was quenching the truth about grace.

Now, however, the proverbial pendulum has swung the other way, and often the opposite is true: The fact that you struggle to stay sober doesn't mean you can't keep ministering to the youth in your home. Although you've battled the desire to sleep around on your wife or are addicted to pornography, it doesn't mean you have to give up your position as a deacon or an elder. Today, the reality of acceptance through grace—which is good—can be so overemphasized that it mutes any discussion about the need to be accountable for our sins. That's a dangerous and unbiblical mistake. We are forgetting that *our behavior is a direct reflection of the health of our relationship with God.* And although I will be the first to admit that it is not an easy task, the church (myself included) needs to learn more about balancing discipline and grace.

Everybody Recognizes a Tourist

If you've ever been out of your home country, you know what it's like to be a foreigner. It's humbling. The way you talk and act stands out as different from everyone else. I remember my last experience as a foreigner when I visited India. My language was different. My clothes were different. The money in my pockets was different. And the way I seasoned my rice and vegetables was *extremely* different! I was a foreigner in that country, and I'm 100 percent sure no one mistook me for a native.

Is the same true of us as Jesus' followers today? Are onlookers 100 percent sure that our lives look nothing like the lives of the rest of the world? That's a difficult question to answer. I'm not talking about hairstyles, clothes, or Toyota Camrys. I'm talking about speech, character, and being last. On one hand, we can never know for sure what people are thinking. On the other hand, we can make an educated guess. We've all heard comments and criticisms of our actions. Each of us has a reputation. What's yours like? Do people say, "You certainly have a different philosophy about money; you don't seem to have any trouble giving it away." Or "You should start thinking about yourself more." Or "It's weird how you don't seem to be bitter or angry about the disappointments in your life." If you hear comments like these, congratulations. Chances are, you're a foreigner.

If you don't hear comments like these, why not? Could it be that your life has become a mirror image of the average individual on planet Earth? Could it be that you've copied "the behavior and customs of this world"? In any case, your actions tell the world to whom you belong. Your actions either make you blend in with everybody else, or they cause people to wonder why you stand out and whether it has something to do with Jesus Christ. Which is it for you?

Warning! Warning!
After Peter urges us to be "temporary residents and foreigners," he gives a warning that we would do well to heed: "Keep away

from worldly desires that wage war against your very souls." This isn't a casual piece of advice that Peter merely mentions in passing—it's a life and death matter, an issue of ultimate reward or everlasting regret. It is a true *warning*. If you don't watch out for the evil desires that creep into your heart and manipulate your actions, you will lose the very foundation of who you are. In essence, you will rot.

I still remember a do-or-die warning I received when I was a freshman at Columbia International University. Back then, the last thing I cared about was others. I'd made it to college, and it was time to reward myself with the freedoms I thought I deserved after having spent eighteen years under someone else's authority. It was time for *me* to be first. I didn't care that I had signed an agreement with the Bible college to follow specific behavioral guidelines. The only thing I cared about was whatever little whim crept into my selfish skull. I was known to skip chapel and class and sometimes stayed out past curfew. I broke the dress code. I was loud and disruptive in the library and student center.

All of these were infractions of the agreement of honor I had signed, but I didn't care. I had no intention of being last! I wasn't going to put the institution, the faculty and staff, and other students before myself. Some in leadership asked why I had come to school there if I didn't care about the college's motto, "To Know Him and Make Him Known." But I told them I loved Jesus and asked them to give me another chance. They exuded the ideal balance of discipline and grace.

Soon after my reprieve, I became restless and plotted a new prank that was sure to enliven the campus. My friend Sling had found two translucent masks that gave the hybrid impression of Jason from *Friday the 13th* and Hannibal Lecter. Naturally, we felt obligated to put them to use. It would not be good stewardship to let such treasures lie dormant in some dorm-room drawer! That night, as we looked out our windows, we noticed a group of guys playing basketball beneath the lights. We grinned when it dawned on us that at some point, the players would have to turn off the lights. That may not sound like a big deal to you, but the switch for the court lights was located far away from the court on the edge of a thickly wooded area. Whoever came to shut off the lights was going to experience the fear of God in a very real way!

Dressed in black, we donned the masks. Then we got carried away and added some other props: a plastic knife for Sling and a fake ax for me. That was a mistake. By the time we scampered out to the woods, we had missed the guys turning out the lights. Our initial plan was foiled, but not to worry. We would invent something on the fly.

Almost immediately we spotted two joggers on the long road leading into campus. I didn't know who they were or how they would react, but I told Sling we should stand completely still and quiet in the middle of the road and show off the masks and weaponry when the joggers got close enough.

As they approached, I knew that we were about to give them a cardiovascular workout like they'd never experienced before. What we didn't know was that these runners were young women. About fifteen yards away, the girls slowed down and one called out in a sweet, quivering tone, "Who is that?" All she got in return were moonlit flashes of an enormous knife and the head of an ax. Again she called out, "Who is that?" This time we took a few steps toward them. That was all it took to quadruple their pulse rates and send them bolting into the night, screaming as they ran toward the nearby home—of the dean of women!

With our work done, we headed back to the dorms, only to come upon two guys along the way. We couldn't leave *them* alone and then be accused of playing sexist pranks. So we decided to run up on each side of them, walking and talking aggressively, weapons in our hands. Needless to say, they were both frightened and irritated by our attempt at late-night companionship. We laughed all the way back to the dorms.

The next day I received a phone call from the dean of men, who had received a phone call from the dean of women. Apparently, my reputation for mischief was growing among the faculty and staff. The dean of men called me to his office and informed me that the previous night's activities had been the last straw: The vice president had made an executive decision to expel me from school.

It was then that I realized I had no regard for anyone around me. Instead of following the college's motto of knowing Jesus and making him known, I had adopted my own motto: "Know Jeremy and Make Him Known." My actions had been far from Christlike, and the administrators at the college saw no reason for me to continue my education at an institution that put such a high value on meekness, humility, and being last.

It wasn't the pranks necessarily, or the sloppy clothes I wore, or the way I slouched in chapel. It was my heart.

Miraculously, the dean of men appealed the vice president's ruling and gave me one more chance. Now, *that's* grace and mercy. He believed there was something in me that could still be set on fire for Jesus. Several weeks later it happened. During chapel I was sitting in the balcony, where, like many freshmen, I normally just goofed around. But on that day I got hooked on a guy's message about the Crucifixion. He was expounding on

Isaiah 53, explaining how Jesus was physically brutalized for our sin and describing the step-by-step torture he endured. The message zeroed in on Jesus' putting the Father and people before himself. It was the ultimate act of being last.

The speaker described, at each step along the way, how my sin had caused Christ's trauma. My cheating led to his beating. My malice and abuse of other people could be linked to the thirty-nine lashes that ripped the skin off his back. My lust and hatred caused the crown of thorns to be pressed into his head.

When the speaker told of Christ being nailed to the cross for my sinful whims, I began to envision the process. I could see the soldier with his hammer, driving spikes into Jesus' hands and feet. I seemed to feel the searing pain shooting through his body. Then I "saw" the soldier swinging the hammer, and my face was reflected on his helmet. My whole world came to a halt at the stunning realization of what the Crucifixion really meant. It had been a while since I had thought about how my sin makes Jesus feel and about my role in Christ's death. *My actions* caused his pain. His pain provided me with the freedom to change, to find forgiveness, and to escape the punishment I deserved. My recent life had been a slap in the face to God.

I wept uncontrollably.

As I read Peter's command to "keep away from worldly desires that wage war against your very souls," I remember this defining event in my life and I see clearly how Jesus took my pain upon himself so that I could experience the very deepest soul satisfaction available to humanity. He was setting me free to follow new desires that would quench the thirst inside. Instead of chasing my corrupted desire to be the most important person on the planet, only to find that my soul was slowly being killed off in the process, I could now find true life—abundant life—as an alien and foreigner in this world. Where is *your* true allegiance—with God or with the world?

[Jesus said,] If you try to hang on to your life, you will lose it. But if you give up your life for my sake, you will save it.

MATTHEW 16:25

They See How *You* Live

Often, our motivation for living is based ultimately on how it affects us. If making people happy gives us a better reputation, then we make people happy. If making God happy makes us feel better about ourselves, then we aim to please God. If forgetting everyone else and acting on the first thing that pops into our minds makes us happy, then that's what we do. In each of these options we are careful how we live, but *we* are the real beneficiaries of those actions. However, Peter's command to "be careful" is defined differently.

Notice the relationship of "you" and "they" in 1 Peter 2:12: "Be careful to live properly among *your* unbelieving neighbors. Then even if *they* accuse *you* of doing wrong, *they* will see *your* honorable behavior, and *they* will give honor to God when he judges the world" (emphasis added).

Peter wants us to live carefully like temporary residents and foreigners so that people get a glimpse of how to honor God. Although we may reap many personal benefits from obeying God both now and in the future, we must not focus on ourselves, because our actions can have saving value for those in the world around us. The more we look like Jesus instead of like the world, the more opportunities we give people to find access to the God for whom their soul longs. When you honor God in the way you behave, God can teach others to do the same through your example. Your life can have everlasting benefits when *"they* see how *you* live."

The Jesus Hug

It's not difficult to recall moments when my changed attitude and actions have allowed people to see Jesus in contrast to the common ways of the world. But I want to tell you about a sin issue I personally struggled with when I was growing up, and also how God helped me to overcome it through learning to be last. When I was a teenager, I struggled with hating gay people. When the topic came up in conversation, I was the first person to crack a joke or talk about how "they all need a good beating to knock some sense into them." I didn't think about homosexuals as people with personal histories and human needs; I thought of them as freaks who warranted my wisecracks, malice, and phobia.

One day I was listening to a song by Steve Camp about people with AIDS dying around the world. The song described God's brokenness over the suffering of his created children. One line in particular stood out: "These are souls that he suffered for." When I connected those words to the gay community suffering with AIDS, I experienced an epiphany, a revelation. I realized that God's concern and compassion for human beings did not stop when it came to homosexuals.

Christ's act on the cross was designed for *every kind of sinner.* I knew homosexuality was wrong, but I had no right to think of myself as better than anyone else just because someone else's sin was different from mine. The Bible commands us to hate sin (see Romans 12:9), yes, but Jesus loves sinners. If I was going to follow Jesus, then I would need to learn to embrace *all people* in hopes of guiding them toward a loving God who could help.

I could not exclude anyone, because *God did not exclude me!*

A while back I was preaching at a church in Atlanta when God gave me a chance to redeem myself for my earlier years of bigotry. At the end of the evening service a middle-aged man made his way toward me the moment I stepped off the stage. I immediately guessed from his mannerisms that he was gay. That lingering stereotype stirred an uneasy feeling in me, and the fact that I even had that reaction shamed me.

As the man drew closer, he began to open his arms in preparation for a hug. My mind raced. Should I step back? Give him a fake, obligatory hug? Should I be last? I didn't want to hurt his feelings or make him feel uncomfortable, so I embraced him with the warmth I thought Christ would give. I was thinking, *I did it! I'm learning, I'm growing. This is great!* Then he kissed me on the cheek. (Now *that* took me out of my comfort zone!)

I was in shock. Struggling to continue to put him first, I prayed. Then he said these words: "I'm so glad you came back to this church. I have wanted to say thank you for a year now. The last time you came, a friend of mine from the church invited me to attend. At the time, I was gay and homeless, living on the streets. That night, I got saved after your message. I have been with the church ever since. Now I'm not gay, and God has given me a home. I just want to say thank you."

My insides melted. There I was, struggling over the embrace, and he had come to thank me for the small part I had played in his relationship with Jesus Christ. I cannot tell you how glad I am that God had changed my heart and is continuing to do so. I would never have been able to give my brother in Christ that

Jesus hug if it weren't for the earlier nudge toward Christlikeness. That man had experienced enough of the world's exclusion. He didn't need more of the world from me! He needed a Jesus hug so that together we could celebrate his new life in Christ, just for a moment. Being last that day—putting another man's needs ahead of my own uneasiness—turned out to be an enormous blessing.

One Step Closer

Up to this point, we've been talking about the contrast between looking like Christ and looking like the world, but in reality, there are *not* two cut-and-dried options of how to live your life: like Christ or like the world. There is actually a long continuum between the two. That's why I want to emphasize becoming *more* like Christ instead of being *completely* like him. It's a vast spectrum, and we don't normally jump from one end to the other in a day. Lifestyle and character changes take time. When you plant a seed in the ground, you don't expect to see a giant tree the next day. The same is true when you're on the road to becoming last.

I think a better way to evaluate how you are living your life is to imagine your rating scale like the alphabet. Imagine the twenty-six letters of the English alphabet lined up from A to Z. Let's call A your conversion (justification)—the time you felt deep sorrow over your sins, realized you had hurt God, asked forgiveness, and committed yourself to living God's way. That was the moment God declared you "not guilty." This decision set you on the journey from A to Z. Let's call Z heaven, and let's call Y Christlikeness. Heaven is our final hope, but Christlikeness is our goal on earth.

Remember, during our journey we can't jump from B to J or even from *B* to *D*. Growth and maturity take time and involve a number of complex factors. Spiritual growth (sanctification) is just like physical growth or mental growth. No one goes from being four feet tall to six feet tall in a day, a week, a month, or even a year. Similarly, no one becomes an expert in a particular field without years of education. We should not expect anything different on our journey toward Christlikeness. It takes time, and there will be massive challenges along the way. We'll need to create some nourishing life habits. We hope that there will be godly mentors and deep Bible study, and certainly there will be tough choices. But reaching the goal—*Z*, for heaven—will be worth it all. Your life will have been well worth living. Not only will you benefit from each letter you reach along the way, but "they" will as well when "they see how you live."

When you look at life one letter at a time, you become more aware of the growth God is birthing within you. I can see the steps I've taken, from hating homosexuals to embracing them as Jesus would. You will notice how your attitudes have changed, from blurting out a complaint when you walk in the door at home, to offering a loving comment to the first person you encounter. You begin to be aware of these small steps that are moving you along the lengthy continuum toward Christlikeness.

As you look at life by the letter, you also become more tuned in to periods of stagnancy. You recognize those times when you seem to have put aside all efforts to change and have begun to fall into your old selfish habits. It's helpful to ask yourself periodically, *What letter am I on? How long have I been here?* Your honest answers will help you to determine whether you are looking more and more like Jesus—or more and more like the world. If you've been on the same letter for a long time, take stock of your behavior, and determine the next move you can make to move yourself along toward greater Christlikeness.

A Square Peg in a Round Hole?

All of us want to fit in somewhere, but *we* must decide where. Do you want to fit in with other Jesus imitators, or do you want to fit in with the world? You can't do both.

In my conversations with people I meet, they often mention new, edgy songs or the latest controversial box-office hit at the movies. When I tell them I'm not familiar with the song or movie to which they're referring, they are flabbergasted. "You need to get out more," they say. "You don't know what you're missing!" Such feedback used to embarrass me, but now it encourages me, because I see it as confirming my citizenship. I'm not from here. I'm a part of Jesus' dream for human life, and that doesn't always mesh with the world's system, philosophy, interests, or dynamics.

I've found that the more time you spend getting to know Jesus and imitating the way he acts, the less time you have to get involved with the world. Now, I'm by no means suggesting that you sit in your room all day saying no to everything and everyone and not reading *USA Today* or watching *24* or *Extreme Makeover: Home Edition*. On the contrary, I'm suggesting that you start investing yourself in God's mission every day of every week. Ask him for wisdom in this. Believe me, you'll be busy, and suddenly you'll have run out of time to waste on what the world offers.

Right about now, you may be ready to protest what I've just said and think that I'm supporting the kind of "holy huddle" mentality that advocates pulling away from the world and into some isolated Christian bubble. Trust me, I'm not advocating a disappearance from society. I love a good basketball game as much as—maybe more than—the next guy. But I am trying to be an advocate of Jesus' approach to life and the values he passed on to us. Did he hang out with sinners? Yes. Did he go to their homes and eat and talk with them? Yes, he did. But that's not the end of the story. He hung out with sinners in order to share God's love with them and to give them the chance to see who he was. He embraced them with a message of repentance and forgiveness and called them to change and to live life his way.

It's all about your motives. If your true motive is to hang out in non-Christian crowds to show Jesus to the world, then go for it. Rely on the power of Christ as you pray and witness and demonstrate the compassion and love of God for all to see. But if your motive is to hang out in non-Christian crowds because those people and what they're doing appeals to your flesh, you need to bolt for the exit. Those motives are a one-way road to blending in with the world. Trust me, your witness will lose its meaning, and your salt will lose its savor. Don't let that happen.

I've been around the block enough to say with confidence that people who don't love Jesus will never spur you on to the next letter, the one that makes you more like Christ. Instead, they will try to pull you down to their lowest common denominator so that they aren't forced to struggle with the God to whom your life is pointing them.

God has given you a life to live and has laid out a blueprint for it in the person of Jesus. If you want to be a good steward of God's property (you) and let your life be an example to others of how they should live, then map out your move to the next letter. The journey away from the world and toward Christlikeness is challenging, but the benefits for you and for those God puts in your path will far outweigh the difficulties.

And the truth is, the more out of place you feel on earth, the more perfectly you'll fit in at your home to come. Make the choice to be last, to enjoy life as a foreigner. And bring along as many sojourners as possible to your final destination.

8

The Cover-Up

"Being Last" by Living a Life of Confession

Someone once said that "a man with a passion rides a wild horse." How true it is. When our lives are "all about me," we're on a slippery slope, a dangerous road on which it's impossible to be last. We get so fixated on ourselves and our selfish ambitions that we can become deceived about our sin and even callous about it. We end up doing things we never imagined we would do, and in the process, we find ourselves spinning out of control and far from God and his desires for our lives. Let me offer an illustration.

Many of us have at least one friend whose life seems to be dictated by Murphy's Law, which says that whatever *can* go wrong *will* go wrong. It even happened to a sweet girl named Jenny. When Jenny entered her freshman year of high school, she set her mind on becoming a track star, not because of the advice of her parents, teachers, or closest friends who saw great promise in her athletic ability. Nor did she have a fire in her belly to represent the United States in the Olympic Games. Her motivation far exceeded such mundane considerations: She was out to make an impression on a boy.

Day in and day out Jenny worked, practiced, sweat, trained,

and prepared for her track debut in front of the upperclassman who had captured her heart. She chose the 110-meter hurdle as the race that would win his attention. It was a dicey choice that tapped not only her sprinting ability but also her timing and pace as she attempted to leap over four hurdles directly in front of the stands.

When the big day arrived, Jenny was confident and relaxed. She had mastered the technique and believed her chances for victory were solid. Readying herself for the gun, she scanned the crowd. There he was, in the middle of the stands, one of the most popular guys in the senior class. Jenny couldn't wait to show him how gifted she was. Then the unexpected happened.

From the crowd of excited spectators came the voice of the young man: "You can do it, Jenny!"

Suddenly, Jenny went dizzy as she pictured herself dating the most popular senior in school. She would be the envy of every girl in her class! She glanced up at him and saw him smiling. By that point, she had entered a dream world.

Then the gun sounded.

They were off, but Jenny, in a daze, was a step behind the other runners. At the first hurdle, she shot straight up in the air and came down on top of the hurdle, scraping her legs. Continuing on pure adrenaline, she duplicated her first jump on the second hurdle, scraping her body again. By the time she got to the third hurdle, the crowd was screaming for her to stop.

As Jenny glanced toward the stands to figure out what to do, she ran directly into the third hurdle and slammed her whole body to the ground. This time she did not—could not—get up, until her friends dragged her to the infield. Jenny's brief track career came to an abrupt end.

Her desire had been to make an impression, and she did. I'm writing about Jenny, not because she was an example of grace in motion that day but because she was the quintessential portrait of a person who did not know how to give up until she had completely fallen apart. It happens to all of us. We get carried away on a path that is going to ruin us, but because we insist on being first, we ignore the warning signs along the way. One fall leads to another until we find ourselves flat on our faces. The only difference is that the stakes are much higher when we're talking about sin.

The first step in being last is recognizing our selfish ambitions, owning up to them, and then renouncing them, because as long as we are set on being first instead of last, we'll never experience what it feels like to be used by God in the way he wants to use us.

A Man after God's Heart

King David was a humble man, yet for a season in his life, he put himself and his desires above God. His is the perfect—or should I say, most disastrous—example of how, when it comes to selfish ambition, one screwup can lead to another, and another, all the way to a complete moral breakdown. The story begins innocently enough, on a breezy, late-spring afternoon in Jerusalem:

In the spring of the year, when kings normally go out to war, David sent Joab and the Israelite army to fight the Ammonites. They destroyed the Ammonite army and laid siege to the city of Rabbah. However, David stayed behind in Jerusalem.

Late one afternoon, after his midday rest, David got out of bed and was walking on the roof of the palace. As he looked out over the city, he noticed a woman of unusual beauty taking a bath. He sent someone to find out who she was, and he was told, "She is Bathsheba, the daughter of Eliam and the wife of Uriah the Hittite." Then David sent messengers to get her; and when she came to the palace, he slept with her. She had just completed the purification rites after having her menstrual period. Then she returned home.   2 SAMUEL 11:1-4

When we bump into David in this account, we don't find him working hard for justice in the kingdom of Israel or composing a new psalm recounting the great things God had done for him. He's taking a snooze. The author of the account takes special care to portray David as somewhat irresponsible, if not lazy. In fact, the writer has deliberately included verse 1, perhaps to demonstrate David's neglect of his royal responsibilities. Let me explain.

In Israel there were essentially two seasons—the dry season, from spring to fall, and the wet season, predominantly in winter. The dry season, which was much more conducive to fighting battles, became known as the time of year when kings go to war. It usually began in spring and lasted until harvest, when every able-bodied man would be needed at home to help in the fields.

Although the kings of that era appointed military commanders who could handle field operations if a king was called away from battle in an emergency, the kings were the ultimate commanders of their armies and maintained a close connection with their fighting forces through their courageous and skillful leadership on the battlefield. In this account, however, the text makes it clear that during Israel's siege of the city Rabbah (the ancient capital of Ammon, just forty miles east of Jerusalem), David had stayed behind at his palace. If there was some critical matter affecting Israel's home front, the writer made no mention of it. Instead, we find David waking up from a nap and taking a stroll on the rooftop. Instead of functioning as an able leader who goes where he is most needed, David appears to be kicking back and basking in the comforts of his royal position.

When Personal Desire Takes the Driver's Seat

To better understand the context for this account, we need to remember that David was married. Anytime he wanted to enjoy the physical pleasures of married life, he could. But on the day in question, it seems that was not enough for the king. As he paced on the rooftop, he spotted Bathsheba, who was also married.

Bathsheba's father, Eliam, and her husband, Uriah the Hittite, were some of the most loyal soldiers in David's army. The Bible even includes them among David's "mighty men," members of the king's elite force. Ahithophel, Eliam's father and Bathsheba's grandfather, was one of David's most trusted advisors (see 2 Samuel 15:12; 16:23). So David may have had some idea of whose house he was eyeballing when he looked down from his palace roof. In any event, he saw an exceptionally attractive woman and wanted her.

What *should* David have done? The ideal response would have been to acknowledge her beauty, bury his desires, and promptly walk away. Put God first. Make himself last. But instead, David did what so many of us do: He began to toy with the possibilities. He continued filling his eyes with her beauty. Slowly it began to escape him that he was flirting with disaster.

David made the critical mistake of entertaining his lust,

letting it smolder, allowing it to build, and thinking only of himself. The lust and sin progressed, and soon David was sending a servant to find out the woman's identity. But his inquiry was not the result of idle curiosity. He needed to find out whether there would be any ramifications if he pursued Bathsheba. He wanted to know whether another man (a husband) would get in the way of his sexual impulse, which is no surprise, since that is where lust always leads its undisciplined followers. Lust is always characterized by the desire for immediate gratification, and David's desire was no different—even when he learned about Bathsheba's close connections to his honorable friends and loyal fighters.

We all know what this internal magnet of desire—the "now factor"—feels like. For some people, it's similar to what happens when I see certain foods. A calzone with red sauce, a juicy steak, chocolate-chip ice cream, and a Wisconsin bratwurst all produce powerful cravings. I can't even pass the cookie aisle in the grocery store without walking away with a package of Nutter Butter cookies in one hand and Oreos with Double Stuf in the other. It doesn't matter whether those cookies cost five dollars and lack any trace of unprocessed, natural ingredients. I don't buy them for that. I buy them because I *must*—because my taste buds have temporarily taken the place of my brain.

Others of us have the same kind of physiological-emotional response when we see a certain pair of shoes or an outfit that seems to have been designed just for us. The thought of the perfect fit or brilliant match or flattering cut somehow severs the mental pathway to the mathematical-financial part of the brain that might have weighed the potential damage to our bank accounts, and we begin to declare aloud, "I have to have it, have to have it." Of course, you didn't "have to have it" a minute before, when you didn't know it existed, but now everything has changed. There is one overriding desire, and it must be satisfied—*now*. The success of future social engagements hangs in the balance. Me first!

That's exactly what happened to King David. His lust for Bathsheba overcame him, and he had to have her. Without the crippling effect of lust, David could have thought about the boundaries God had set for relationships, about the marriage vows David had taken, about the honorable men in Bathsheba's family—even about the possibility that Bathsheba could become pregnant. Let's dwell just on this last possibility for a moment.

The text explicitly informs us (v. 4) that Bathsheba had just completed the required purification rights required of all women on the eighth day following their menstrual period. This meant that she was at a point when she would be most likely to conceive. Every Israelite woman went through the same process, so if David's desire had not disabled his analytical abilities, he might have figured out that giving in to his sexual desires for a woman at that particular time would have been a most dangerous maneuver for a man wanting to hide his actions.

But David wasn't thinking rationally. He made no attempt to reason logically, let alone give any consideration to God's wishes. Lust had taken over. That's why, when the word came back that Bathsheba's husband was one of the king's elite operatives, David's conscience wasn't the least bit roused. The news meant only that the important men in Bathsheba's life were off to battle, and David could get on with satisfying his desires! Indeed, a man with a passion rides a wild horse, and so King David sent for Bathsheba.

One Look, Then Book!

At this point, David stands as a perfect example of how *not* to handle sexual impulses. He chose the "I do what I feel" route. He decided that living life God's way wasn't as important as satisfying his own desires. If God's way had been a priority for David, he would have bolted after the first glance. He would have been thinking, *Be last.* He would have run to his throne room and scheduled a domestic-policy meeting or set out to check on his army's progress in the east—anything to get his mind off the lust raging within.

At the least David could have dusted off his harp and sung one of the psalms he had penned, Psalm 119:9, for example: "How can a young person stay pure? By obeying your word." He could have put a halt to his downward spiral if he had taken the kind of defensive stance against sin that Jesus talked about. Look at his words regarding the seventh commandment:

> You have heard the commandment that says, "You must not commit adultery." But I say, anyone who even looks at a woman with lust has already committed adultery with her in his heart. So if your eye—even your good eye—causes you to lust, gouge it out and throw it away. It is better for you to lose one part of your body than for your whole body to be thrown into hell. And if your hand—even your stronger hand—causes you to sin, cut it off and throw it away. It is better for you to lose one part of your body than for your whole body to be thrown into hell. MATTHEW 5:27-30

There's no way around it; this is serious business. Jesus uses a hyperbole (an exaggeration for effect) to grab our attention about how dangerous a glance can become. Although he isn't promoting self-inflicted injury, he paints this visual picture to warn us about how deadly the "do what you feel" mentality can be. Having eyes that run quickly to lust is worse than having no eyes at all.

When have your eyes crossed the line and entered into the realm of "adultery"? The first glance is always just an innocent observation of what or who is around us. But the *second* look is different. When we continue to look, ponder the possibilities, and take note of shapes and sizes, *that's* when it becomes dangerous. We find ourselves on the fast track to dismantling the beautiful way God designed us to relate to one another. It's a corrupt state of mind. When we make ourselves last, we flee youthful lusts. But when we make ourselves first, we run quickly to lust and often find ourselves needing to sin more to cover up our tracks, just as David did.

David took a first glance, then a long second look. That second look led to an affair with Bathsheba. A few weeks after the one-night fling, David got a message that his sexual quick fix had some big-time consequences:

> When Bathsheba discovered that she was pregnant, she sent David a message, saying, "I'm pregnant." Then David sent word to Joab: "Send me Uriah the Hittite." So Joab sent him to David. When Uriah arrived, David asked him how Joab and the army were getting along and how the war was progressing. Then he told Uriah, "Go on home and relax." David even sent a gift to Uriah after he had left the palace. But Uriah didn't go home. He slept that night at the palace entrance with the king's palace guard. 2 SAMUEL 11:5-9

Bathsheba was pregnant, and in David's attempt to cover it up, any semblance of his "sound mind" went on a road trip, and an unfathomable turn of events unfolded. In short, David's plan to have Uriah sleep with Bathsheba in order to account for her pregnancy failed. Have you ever tried to cover up your sin only to watch your best-laid plans fall apart before your eyes? I have.

I devised one of my greatest cover-up schemes in the days of my youth. The scene was a Wisconsin cornfield on my parents' property. I had the task of planting seed in careful rows and then covering the seed with rich, dark Midwest soil. I got off to a good start and knocked out the first half before lunch. With the help of Mom's country cooking, I recharged and went back to finish the day. But soon I became overwhelmed and frustrated with the amount of work still left to do. I had things to do and people to see. And I had better ideas about how to spend my Saturday than with a shovel and a wheelbarrow.

Pooling my frustration and my desire to get out of that cornfield, I devised a plan that would enable me to plant all the seed and still be done in time to have some fun. I would simply dump the rest of the seed in one area, kick the dirt around, and give it the true "look" of a carefully planted cornfield. I was done in no time. (When parents tell their children, "You can't play until you get your chores done," the children just might translate it, "Please figure out a way to do a poor job on your chores.")

When I arrived back at the house with a smile and a declaration that I had finished the project, my mom took a quick look at the field and then asked, "Did you really plant all the corn already?"

Fortunately for me, she had phrased the question in such a way that I could answer "honestly." "Why, yes, I did plant all the corn." Sure I had. I had created a massive stockpile of corn, which was now covered with fertile soil. During the next few weeks I often wondered what my parents thought as an enormous bunch of cornstalks emerged from the depths of the field. I, for one, was rather proud of supplanting the tale of "Jack and the Beanstalk" with "Jeremy and the Cornstalks," but when my parents called me outside in order to "show me something," my pride quickly morphed into fear. After silently walking me out to the world's largest corn "clump", they simply asked, "What is that?"

It was all over. The plan I had devised to cover my rebellion had failed. I briefly contemplated hatching another great lie to try to get myself off the hook, but there was no point in denying what I had done. My sin was evident.

Hide at All Costs

If only David had given up on his cover-up attempt when Uriah refused to go home to Bathsheba, a man's life could have been saved. David could have put an end to the downward spiral of his sin, but fear of the consequences of his adultery motivated him to even greater depths of deceit. David had become used to putting himself first. He would try another scheme to save his skin, even though he knew deep down that his actions would become all the more offensive to God.

When David heard that Uriah had not gone home, he summoned him and asked, "What's the matter? Why didn't you go home last night after being away for so long?" Uriah replied, "The Ark and the armies of Israel and Judah are living in tents, and Joab and my master's men are camping in the open fields. How could I go home to wine and dine and sleep with my wife? I swear that I would never do such a thing." "Well, stay here today," David told him, "and tomorrow you may return to the army." So Uriah stayed in Jerusalem that day and the next. Then David invited him to dinner and got him drunk. But even then he couldn't get Uriah to go home to his wife. Again he slept at the palace entrance with the king's palace guard.

2 SAMUEL 11:10-13

Is it a sin to get drunk? Yes. Is it a sin to get other people drunk? Yes. Jesus said, "What sorrow awaits the world, because it tempts people to sin. Temptations are inevitable, but what sorrow awaits the person who does the tempting" (Matthew 18:7). These straightforward words from Jesus should be terrifying to anyone who leads someone else into sin. David intentionally played the role of tempter. To cover up his own sin, he coaxed Uriah into sin.

Have you ever caused someone else to sin? I have, and I'm not proud of it. In fact, I still feel convicted about it. When you lead someone else into sin, do you care? Do you take seriously Jesus' commands to set a good example for others? Do you believe him when he says that "sorrow awaits the person who does the tempting"?

In putting his own desires first, David ignored the warnings of God and fell further and further away from reality.

Sin's Slippery Slope

Jesus taught that we should love God with all our heart, soul, mind, and strength and love our neighbors as ourselves (see Luke 10:27). He said that if we did this, we would be obeying all of his commandments. That's because when we truly love God and our neighbors and put their interests above our own, then we don't lie, steal, covet, murder, or commit adultery, because we care about

Jesus—and other people—too much to do those things. In other words, we care too much about being last to do those things.

But in this tragic episode, David did not put God and others first; he put himself above all others. When cover-up number one didn't work and cover-up number two fell short, he hoped the third time would be the charm. The next morning, David wrote a letter to Joab at the front lines and gave it to Uriah to deliver. The letter gave the following instructions to Joab: "Station Uriah on the front lines where the battle is fiercest. Then pull back so that he will be killed" (2 Samuel 11:15). The message was brief, but shockingly to the point, and it demonstrated just how far David would go to cover up his sin. What audacity! He put the length of Uriah's life in his own hands. He played God! He knew the authority he had as king and felt no qualms about abusing it.

To David, this must have seemed like the perfect plan. Uriah would die, and David would take Uriah's widow (his new lover) as his wife. The community would love David for it. ("Isn't it great that David is going to take in the new widow? What a sensitive king we have, who thinks so much about others!") If David's plan worked, he would get it all: the husband out of the picture, the girl, the sex, his reputation intact—and no one would ever know the truth!

I wonder what was going through David's mind when he wrote that letter to Joab, putting into motion a plan that would surely result in Uriah's death. Some scholars believe that a short time before this, David had written these words: "O LORD, our Lord, your majestic name fills the earth! Your glory is higher than the heavens. . . . When I look at the night sky and see the work of your fingers—the moon and the stars you set in place—what are mere mortals that you should think about them, human beings that you should care for them?" (Psalm 8:1, 3-4).

Did David compose the words of that psalm, sentences that would be recorded for all time in God's holy Word, and then with the same "pen" write the letter that would lead to a murder so he could cover up his sin? *Wow!*

At first, the scenario played out just as David had hoped. Uriah delivered his own death warrant to Joab and lost his life in the next battle near the walls of Rabbah. Then a messenger brought David news of his army's apparent failure—but his secret success.

The report of the battle's disastrous results pushed the hardhearted David even deeper into his cover-up. When he had heard the messenger's full report, he responded with cloaked words: "'Well, tell Joab not to be discouraged,' David said. 'The sword devours this one today and that one tomorrow! Fight harder next time, and conquer the city!'" (2 Samuel 11:25). *What?* How could David lie through his teeth and account for such a disaster with fleeting words about the collateral damage of war? What had happened to him? He was the poetic teacher of the law. He had written and sung songs about God's salvation and righteousness. He was the political leader of a nation created to reflect God's glory to others. But David had become the epitome of "self."

These are the consequences of being first. David had fallen down sin's slippery slope. What had started as an appreciative glance at feminine beauty on a rooftop ended with adultery, deception, and murder.

How could that happen to a "man after God's heart"? It happened one wrong step at a time. David's laziness led to lust. His lust took action in the form of an inquiry. His inquiry resulted in sexual sin. From there, his desire to save face resulted in lies, drunkenness, and murder.

We aren't immune to the danger of this slippery slope. In order to save our own spiritual reputations, we, too, try to bury our sins. We may reason that because of our position in the church or our level of involvement in ministry, it would be better to cover up our sins than to confess them. But how much more sin do we add to our lives through the deception required to hide it? I suspect that the same slippery slope that carried David from lust to murder takes us for a ride more often than we want to admit. So, what can we do to stop it? To start with, we need to take the issues of our own laziness, pride, lust, and selfishness more seriously. The Scriptures tell us,

> Do not love this world nor the things it offers you, for when you love the world, you do not have the love of the Father in you. For the world offers only a craving for physical pleasure, a craving for everything we see, and pride in our achievements and possessions. These are not from the Father, but are from this world. 1 JOHN 2:15-16

The world beckons to us through the desire for physical pleasure or material things, and pride cause us to slide into deception, broken relationships, and sexual sin. The fact is, David was a godly man. He often stopped himself from falling into sin, which goes to show that it takes only one bad decision to put us in the same sewer David found himself in.

The question is, how serious are we willing to get about catching ourselves in the early stages of a sinful slide? Are we willing to talk with a trusted friend or mentor about our areas of weakness? Are we proactive enough to pinpoint the most vulnerable moments in our weekly schedules and then change what we do or with whom we choose to hang out? If the Internet is causing us to sin, are we willing to dramatically reduce the time we spend on it in order to ensure that our minds belong to God? Are we prepared to serve God so continually that we do not have time to get involved in activities that will lead to sin? It's questions like these that we need to be asking ourselves, and answering, in order to halt our own descent on sin's slippery slope.

"You Are That Man!"

After David's slide into the abyss of sin, God sent the prophet Nathan to get David's attention. What did Nathan do to enliven a nagging sense of impropriety in the recesses of David's soul? Well, he didn't immediately call David out, nor did he list how many of God's commandments David had violated. Instead, Nathan chose to creatively reawaken David's residual sense of justice by telling David a story:

> "There were two men in a certain town. One was rich, and one was poor. The rich man owned a great many sheep and cattle. The poor man owned nothing but one little lamb he had bought. He raised that little lamb, and it grew up with his children. It ate from the man's own plate and drank from his cup. He cuddled it in his arms like a baby daughter. One day a guest arrived at the home of the rich man. But instead of killing an animal from his own flock or herd, he took the poor man's lamb and killed it and prepared it for his guest."
>
> David was furious. "As surely as the LORD lives," he vowed, "any man who would do such a thing deserves to die! He must

repay four lambs to the poor man for the one he stole and for having no pity." 2 SAMUEL 12:1-6

David couldn't fathom who in the world would take a lamb from a poor, gentle man when he himself had herds of sheep and cattle on his own property. How blind to justice would someone have to be to justify such an act! It was so blatantly wrong that surely the rich man must have known better. And if he did know better and still took advantage of his fellow man, then he was nothing more than an unrestrained deviant who deserved death.

Then, at the height of David's moral outrage, when his complacency and blurred moral vision had been set back on track momentarily, Nathan turned David's indignation back on himself:

You are that man! The LORD, the God of Israel, says . . . You have murdered Uriah the Hittite with the sword of the Ammonites and stolen his wife. . . . Because of what you have done, I will cause your own household to rebel against you. I will give your wives to another man before your very eyes, and he will go to bed with them in public view. You did it secretly, but I will make this happen to you openly in the sight of all Israel.
2 SAMUEL 12:7, 9-12

In no uncertain terms, Nathan identified David as the man who consciously ignored God's directions and destroyed an innocent man's life. *He* did it. And he would face the consequences.

I don't know exactly what David felt when he heard the rebuke from his faithful friend, but I imagine a large lump formed in his throat, especially when he remembered his words of condemnation toward the rich man who had killed the poor man's prized lamb. His thoughts must have been a whirlwind as his mind replayed images of the rooftop and his personal quarters, where he had lain with Bathsheba and later penned the order for Uriah's death, and then realized the future consequences that God had promised. I can imagine David's pretense melting away and his kingly confidence dissolving into a cringe, as if he had been both longing for and dreading that very moment. I think David's heart was crushed as the weight of his pent-up guilt was released. Perhaps David was recalling these feelings when he penned,

> When I refused to confess my sin, my body wasted away, and I groaned all day long. Day and night your hand of discipline was heavy on me. My strength evaporated like water in the summer heat. PSALM 32:3-4

David had been feeling sin's dreadful effects in the wake of his cover-up. His once free spirit had become heavy, and his joy had turned to an inescapable sense of misery that wore on his soul. It did not take him long to own up to his guilt. In fact, the text tells us that David quickly confessed his sin. Nathan had called him out as "that man," and David readily agreed with what he knew to be true: He had shown disregard for God. He had destroyed a family. He was an adulterer and a murderer. God had given David greatness, and David had used it to make himself first.

The First Step to Restoration Is Always Forgiveness

We've just seen how David responded to Nathan's rebuke. The next question is, how did God respond to David's confession?

> [When David had confessed his sin,] Nathan replied, "Yes, but the LORD has forgiven you, and you won't die for this sin.

Nevertheless, because you have shown utter contempt for the LORD by doing this, your child will die." 2 SAMUEL 12:13-14

David's actions clearly warranted consequences. What he had done reflected poorly on God, and therefore, the observers of this great man of God needed to see clear evidence of God's disapproval. But notice the order of Nathan's words following David's admission of guilt. Immediately after David's confession we *do not* hear God say, "It's over. You've gone too far. I can't take you back, and I can never use you again." Nor does David hear of some great feat God would require of him before he could come back into the fold. There is no such requirement. Instead, the first words David hears Nathan speak are, "The LORD has forgiven you"! Did you get it? The first thing God wanted David to know was that he had been forgiven. Many people understand that sin has consequences, but what many people don't understand is that God loves to forgive! When you confess your sin, God's first response is forgiveness.

Nathan could have reversed the order of his response to David's confession and cited the consequences before the forgiveness, but he did not. His first words were of restoration, affirmation, and tender embracement. David hears "Welcome home, Son" from a compassionate and righteous Father. There was no delay between David's confession and God's forgiveness. No spiritual gymnastics or penitent acts were required for God's favorable disposition to return. Remember the Prodigal Son in the New Testament? What else would we expect from "the God of compassion and mercy" who is "slow to anger and filled with unfailing love and faithfulness" (Exodus 34:6)?

Is It You?

David could have made another run at his cover-up scheme. He could have knocked off Nathan in the hope that in doing so, David's secret would remain a secret. But David's humility and restored sense of right and wrong told him otherwise. "I did it," he said. "I'm sick of covering it up. I sinned, and the buck stops here." In that moment, David's identity changed from Nathan's accusatory label—"that man"—to one of a sinner accepted and redeemed by God—"You have been forgiven."

This story makes David (our Old Testament prodigal) one of my favorite ancestors of the faith. When I need encouragement, I don't think first about the way he passionately worshiped God or performed great acts of faith, such as slaying Goliath. Nor do I first recall his love for God's Word or his ability to treat his greatest enemies with empathy. Instead, it's David's mistakes that get my attention, because I can relate to them. Like David, I sometimes do what I know is wrong, and it causes me to wonder, *How am I* really *doing in my relationship with God?* If I saw a man give orders to kill an innocent man just to protect his spiritual reputation, I would put him at the top of the "no hope" list. But David's life tells me there *is hope.*

Some of David's most admirable character qualities were his meekness, his humility, and his knowledge that God was mighty and magnificent and that without God, David was *nothing.* This awe of the Lord helped David reassume the position of being last, and it's one of the primary characteristics for learning how to be last in our daily lives. Indeed, I believe that at the lowest point in David's spiritual life, God wanted to make a lasting impression on him—the impression of a Father who loved him even when he acted like a barbarian and struck out against the very heart of the

King. I believe God wants to make that same impression on us. He wants to meet us in the rock-bottom moments of our spiritual journeys and provide relief and restoration.

Realizing that *you* are the guilty party at the other end of an accusation like Nathan's does not have to be the end of your story. It can be a new beginning. This is not a time to sulk or try to impress God by doing something twice as good as the bad you did. It is a time to own what you've done. Put your sins on the table, and let Jesus do what he is dying—*has died*—to do! I can't promise you that there won't be consequences, but one of those consequences need not be nagging, guilty feelings, and a broken relationship with your Father.

God's beautiful, instantaneous forgiveness is just one prayer away for those who choose to be last by being quick to confess their sin and then embrace God's incomparable forgiveness.

9

Amazing Jesus

"Being Last" by Living a Life
That Causes Positive Amazement

I see many things in my travels, but at one place I saw one of the most amazing sights of my entire life—the biggest nose on the face of the earth! The thing was huge! This schnoz belongs in the *Guinness Book of World Records*. And I saw it at Mount Rushmore.

Perhaps I enjoyed my time with that nose a little too much. But I just can't help being amazed when I think of the men who spent years and years of their lives sculpting the four gigantic faces that grace the monumental granite sculpture located near Keystone, South Dakota. Think of it. From 1927 to 1941, men with dynamite and sculpting tools risked their lives on the face of a cliff to create likenesses of four of America's presidents: George Washington, Thomas Jefferson, Theodore Roosevelt, and Abraham Lincoln.

What Amazes You?

Perhaps you're amazed by the wonder of the Grand Canyon, a flaming sunset, a snowcapped mountain range, a glorious symphony, or a baby's smile. Indeed, each of these things is amazing. All of them are positive and pleasurable, but sometimes our amazement comes from negative things. I'm still amazed at the hatred that motivated the men who planned and carried out the attack on September 11, 2001.

The point is that certain realities should amaze us one way or another, and if they do not, we probably have yet to grasp the truth about them. Let's bring the concept of amazement into our spiritual lives. The longer I live, the more amazed I am by Jesus. He is our Creator, our Savior, and our Friend. He protects us and appeals to the Father on our behalf. He never stops loving us, no matter what. He *is* amazing! When we contemplate his radical love for us—his unspeakable sacrifice—our amazement turns to thankfulness, awe, and praise. So knowing all these things, can we really continue to put ourselves first? Yes, I'm afraid that we can.

Can Jesus Be Amazed?

What would you say if I told you that the Bible says Jesus can be amazed? You may be thinking, *Wait a minute! If Jesus is God (and I know he is), then he's omniscient. He knows everything. So how could anything amaze him?*

We have to dig deep to answer that question. Two different times the Bible describes Jesus as being amazed: once by something positive and once by something negative. Let's check out those two events in Christ's life. There are treasures to be found and much to be learned in doing so. First, let's look at the event that caused Jesus positive amazement:

> When Jesus returned to Capernaum, a Roman officer came and pleaded with him, "Lord, my young servant lies in bed, paralyzed and in terrible pain."
>
> Jesus said, "I will come and heal him."
>
> But the officer said, "Lord, I am not worthy to have you come into my home. Just say the word from where you are,

and my servant will be healed. I know this because I am under the authority of my superior officers, and I have authority over my soldiers. I only need to say, 'Go,' and they go, or 'Come,' and they come. And if I say to my slaves, 'Do this,' they do it."

When Jesus heard this, he was *amazed*.

MATTHEW 8:5-10 (EMPHASIS ADDED)

In this account, the word *amazed* refers to a *wow!* moment. It is the same word used in Matthew 15:31, where the author describes the astonishment of the crowd after Jesus healed the lame, blind, crippled, and mute. In this text, the Roman officer's response wowed Jesus. The faith that he hoped and expected to find in his own people he found instead in a Roman officer, an unlikely candidate. Jesus was so impressed that he used this man's faith as an example for the crowd: "Turning to those who were following him, he said, 'I tell you the truth, I haven't seen faith like this in all Israel!'" (Matthew 8:10).

These words must have been drastically unsettling for Jesus' Jewish audience. Consider the situation. First, the Roman officer was not a Jew. He did not grow up waiting for the Messiah, who would one day come to earth with the power of the Almighty, nor did he learn to revere the holy writings of the prophets at a synagogue. He was probably more familiar with Graeco-Roman mythology than with the Hebrew Scriptures. By virtue of his military position, he would have been more likely to harass Jesus, a Jewish subject, than to honor him as the One who had power over his servant's health. Yet he showed greater faith than those who had all of God's promises and prophets in their heritage.

Second, the Roman officer wasn't pleading for his own healing. He had not come for himself, or even for a wife, a child, or a parent. He had come on behalf of a servant—a member of the lowest class in Roman society. The officer could probably have bought another servant after his present helper died, but he felt compassion and love for the man who served him. The Scriptures do not tell us why or how that mercy originated. We simply see a Roman officer who has a servant in need and an unwavering belief in Jesus' authority.

Why does this situation make Jesus' amazement even more profound? Because the proud holders of the Scriptures have just been told that a pagan officer from the empire that oppresses them gets it—and *they do not*. The Jews would have reeled at this statement. The officer represented the hated Romans, the very people the Jews despised. He should have been called "unclean" and "unholy," not an example for them to follow. Yet Jesus called him just that.

When I think of this scene and how this man's faith broke through the cultural barriers of first-century Palestine, I can only hope that Jesus sees the same kind of faith in me. Does my faith ever amaze him? It should. That should be as important to me as the amazing One who has given me everything I need in life through his amazing grace.

The Jesus We Never Knew

Now, let's stop for a moment and go back to the idea of God's omniscience. (*Omniscience* is the theological term that describes God's limitless knowledge of all things—past, present, and future.) When we consider the fact that God is omniscient, we realize that he cannot be surprised by anything because he

already knows what will happen. In the case of the Roman officer, Jesus would have known about his faith since before the
beginning of time. So how could Jesus have been amazed?

To answer that question, we need to ask a few others. Did
Jesus ever get angry? Yes. Remember the time he entered the
Temple and found a bunch of racist businessmen cheating people out of money? These men did big business during Passover.
When foreigners came and wanted to change their money into
the Temple currency, the only money accepted for the Temple tax
and the purchase of sacrificial animals, these merchants grossly
inflated the exchange rate and got wealthy doing it. At the same
time, they tried to stop, or at least frustrate, the non-Jewish people who had come to worship. The group wanted to make it clear
that Gentiles were not welcome.

Now, had Jesus not known for all time that these greedy
vendors would be in the Temple courts stealing money intended
for the worship of God? Didn't he know that these people would
try to discourage Gentiles from worshiping him? Of course
he did. But Jesus was so angry at what was going on that he
physically took steps to put these people out of business and
to teach a lesson to those who tried to put a barrier between
people and Jesus:

> Jesus entered the Temple and began to drive out the people
> buying and selling animals for sacrifices. He knocked over the
> tables of the money changers and the chairs of those selling
> doves, and he stopped everyone from using the Temple as a
> marketplace. He said to them, "The Scriptures declare, 'My
> Temple will be called a house of prayer *for all nations.'*"
> MARK 11:15-17 (EMPHASIS ADDED)

Since Jesus knew about all of this ahead of time, why didn't he prepare himself mentally so that he could deal with this issue in a calm, collected manner? He would have had plenty of time. Why did he get so fired up? From a human perspective, at least, the anger that drove Jesus to chase the money changers out of the Gentile court does not seem to correlate with his omniscience.

Let's ask another question: Did Jesus ever cry? Yes. Remember the emotional scene at Lazarus's grave (see John 11) and again when Jesus lamented over Jerusalem (see Matthew 23:37- 39)? If Jesus knew that Lazarus was going to die and then be raised to life again, why would he weep? And if Israel's refusal to follow God and embrace Christ as the Messiah was part of God's eternal knowledge, why would Jesus be brought to tears because they failed to recognize him?

The reason that Jesus could get mad or weep is the same reason why he could be amazed (wowed) at the Roman officer's faith: God has a heart! He feels and cares. This leads us beyond the objective fact of his omniscience into something much deeper, much more passionate. God is not only the God of all knowledge and power. He is also *love*. He invests himself passionately in the lives of men, women, and children, even while knowing exactly how they will choose to live in the future.

Theologians may disagree on certain aspects of the *imago dei* (the image of God), in which we were created, but part of his image in us no doubt includes our emotions. God is not merely some heavenly computer server plugged in to the information superhighway of human events. God is stunningly passionate and emotionally engaged. He can be wounded: "They will recognize how hurt I am by their unfaithful hearts" (Ezekiel 6:9). He can be angry: "The Scriptures declare, 'My Temple will be called a house of prayer *for all nations*'" (Mark 11:17, emphasis added). And he can be amazed: "I tell you the truth, I haven't seen faith like this in all Israel!" (Matthew 8:10).

In light of all we've just seen, it should come as no surprise to us that Jesus was amazed by the resolute faith of an officer in the Roman Imperial Army. God had known for all time that this man would trust his authority, but that in no way lessened his delight and wonder at the man's faith. What he felt there so stood out from his encounters with the Israelites that he had to comment on it!

When I read this biblical account, I wrote in the margin, "I want to amaze Jesus." I want desperately for him to look at the way I live with eyes of amazement. And I am not talking about earning my salvation or gaining points on some righteousness scale. I'm talking about pleasing God and bringing joy to his heart.

The *Worst* Kind of Amazement

Making an impression on God may not always be the best thing if what catches his eye is our independence, our desire to be first and live our own way. Earlier I said that only two times does the Bible talk about Jesus' being amazed. Look what happens when Jesus leaves the western shores of Galilee to go home for a little ministry:

> Jesus left that part of the country and returned with his disciples to Nazareth, his hometown. The next Sabbath he began teaching in the synagogue, and many who heard him were amazed. They asked, "Where did he get all this wisdom and the power to perform such miracles?" Then they scoffed,

"He's just a carpenter, the son of Mary and the brother of James, Joseph, Judas, and Simon. And his sisters live right here among us." They were deeply offended and refused to believe in him.

Then Jesus told them, "A prophet is honored everywhere except in his own hometown and among his relatives and his own family." And because of their unbelief, he couldn't do any miracles among them except to place his hands on a few sick people and heal them. And he was amazed at their unbelief. MARK 6:1-6

Here we meet up with the same word, *amazed*, that we saw in Matthew 8, but in this case, Jesus' amazement reflected a negative slant. He was back in his hometown of Nazareth, and no one was willing to concede that he might be more than just the carpenter they had known him to be. Jesus had family in this town, so even if he was a powerful communicator and a renowned worker of miracles, the townspeople simply refused to accept him as anything more than an oddly talented hometown boy. Jesus was stunned by the dismissive attitude of those people around his old stomping grounds.

Jesus at Half Power?

Let's take a few minutes to contemplate Mark's rather shocking summary statement about Jesus' reaction to the people: "Because of their unbelief, [Jesus] couldn't do any miracles among them except to place his hands on a few sick people and heal them." *What?* Can the Son of God become impotent when it comes to miracles? If he is really God and can do all things (omnipotent), then why couldn't he perform mighty signs and wonders in his hometown?

The text says that Jesus could do some healings but no miracles, "because of their unbelief." So Jesus did retain the ability to perform miracles, but he chose to refrain from performing all the miracles he could have because the people refused to believe he was anything more than a native carpenter. The "what you sow is what you reap" principle comes into play here. Jesus' character would not allow him to graciously bless a community that denied God's presence among them in the person of Jesus the Nazarene.

His decision to perform fewer miracles in Nazareth was not merely the result of cerebral planning. It arose painfully from the disconsolate shock he felt after witnessing the unbelief of the hometown crowd. Even though he knew what to expect all along, it still amazed him in the worst way.

I wonder what he was thinking at the time. Might he have thought, *I've tried and tried and tried to show you who I am? I grew up here. Not once have you seen me sin. Surely you would understand that I am the Messiah. I've tried to reveal that I'm the Savior of the world through my teaching of the prophets. I've tried to express the blessing of God through my sacrificial love for you. And I've tried to demonstrate the power of God through my miraculous deeds. But you just won't take me for who I really am.* Jesus was blown away by their unbelief.

Good Guilt, Bad Guilt

In the same way that Jesus' amazement was positive in one account and negative in the other, the Bible describes a positive kind of guilt and a negative kind of guilt. I want to talk about each of these briefly because when it comes to intimacy in our relationship with Jesus—and with others, for that matter—the bad kind of guilt can hold us back while the good kind can keep us moving forward and growing in our relationship. Let me begin by describing the kind of guilt from which we have all been freed.

Unnecessary guilt is what you feel when you continue to feel bad about sin that you have already confessed to God. God's forgiveness motivates you to change. The Bible calls this *repentance*. No sin for which you have truly repented should continue to haunt you. From God's perspective, feeling guilty over such sin is totally unnecessary and will serve only as a negative, destructive force in your life. That kind of inappropriate guilt is actually fueled by the deceptive thoughts of Satan, whose goal is to discredit the power of the Cross.

A good form of guilt does exist. It's the kind of guilt people feel as a result of sin that has gone unchecked and unaddressed. It's the kind of guilt that weighs heavily on us until we fall on our faces in sorrow before God. This kind of guilt drives us to repentance. It is actually healthy and biblically justified, and it actually works to our benefit. Let me attempt to illustrate the benefit of this good kind of guilt with examples from my own life.

The Garage

For years I've had a dream to restore an old '67 fastback Mustang, and as every dreamer knows, there's no point in going halfway on a good dream. Therefore, my plan is not only to rebuild a finely tuned, tightly detailed automobile. My desire is also to build an upgraded garage to match. The project has begun. The Sheetrock is up, the creases and depressions have been plastered over, and the newly remodeled garage is ready to paint.

For a number of years I worked as a painter. So when it came time to add color to the walls of the garage that would house the most amazing car modern man has ever configured, I would settle for nothing less than the most professional finish. I went straight to Sherwin-Williams. Although I think Sherwin-Williams is the greatest store a painter could ever imagine, apparently not everyone in the nation shares that sentiment. That became obvious when I walked into the store and found absolutely no one in sight except for the guy being paid to stand duty behind the counter.

The average Joe may not bat an eye walking into a situation like that, but when you're an evangelist, sirens sound in your head, your heart rate kicks up a notch, and you begin to pray fervently. Why? Because you have a golden opportunity to direct the conversation toward Christ, with no one there to rush you. This was the textbook example of a prime-time evangelistic opportunity, the kind I describe at evangelism seminars and workshops across the country.

Anyway, I walked up to the counter and read off my list of paint colors and quantities. The attendant and I talked about my detailed plans for both the garage and the car and then reverted to a bit of small talk. Since Christmas was coming, the guy asked if I had my shopping done yet, and I responded affirmatively. He finished mixing the paint, I handed him a good sum of money, and soon I was driving off, eager to get back to my painting project. Several miles down the road, a small but distinct voice from heaven seemed to increase in volume, and I knew for a fact that I had missed an ideal opportunity to share Christ, simply because I had refused to set my selfish dreams and desires aside for a few minutes.

I remembered that in a few days I was scheduled to lead a huge evangelistic training seminar where it was my responsibility to talk about getting the gospel out with passion and about helping people realize how many opportunities we have in our everyday lives to do so. The good kind of guilt arose in my mind, and I couldn't help but ask myself what had gone wrong with me. I'd been leading people to Christ since the fifth grade, and now I had let lesser lusts get in the way of my using the evangelistic gift God had given me. Simply put, I had indulged in a "me first" moment.

If I could pin down and convey God's reaction toward me at that moment, I would say that, yes, he was amazed—in the worst kind of way. That feeling of guilt slowly covered me until my hands trembled. Everything in me reverberated from the sense that the God of all grace was saying to me, *"Wow!* That really hurt. I gave you a chance to touch one of my lost children, and you kept silent. . . . I can't tell you how much that makes my heart ache. I still love you, but that hurt." That "good" guilt bore into the core of my being until I approached the Father in prayer with humble confession. Sure enough, he was merciful and set aflame a new burning to evangelize. In fact, the guy who was helping me paint the garage that day got a solid two-hour dose of the gospel.

My Wife, My Best Friend

Dawn and I have been married since 1994, and we've been "best friends" for just over twenty years. It's the greatest relationship in the world, and I try not to take it for granted. The number of years of friendship actually matter more to me than how long we've been married. You see, anyone can drive down to the courthouse and get a marriage license, but there is no legal document that says "best friends." I consider the companionship I share with Dawn to be a unique and important gift, and I want to preserve it at all costs. We learned early in our marriage that there were a number of things that we did not want to bring into our marriage, either mistakes others had made or ones we had made ourselves. But awhile back, I let a big one back in.

Not long ago, Dawn and I traveled to Washington, D.C., where I lived for a few years when I was growing up. The traffic reflected the hustle and bustle of the nation's capital, and I had to fight to keep pace and stay safe. Everything seemed to be going smoothly as we approached our destination, until I looked at the gas gauge. The low-fuel warning light had come on without my being aware of it. The needle was pointing to "E," and I had no idea how much farther we could drive before we ran out of gas. When the first gas station appeared, I had to cross four lanes of traffic to get there. I cruised around for quite some time before I found a space at a pump. At that point I already wasn't in the best frame of mind, and then, in her sweet, soft voice my wife offered some advice: "Don't forget, the gas goes in on your side."

She thought this information might be of some assistance because we were driving her car on this trip. But her assistance was not going to get a welcome reception from a man who had been fighting traffic for more than two hours.

"I know what side the gas goes in!" I snapped, then exited the car to take care of business.

That exchange might not be a big deal in a lot of marriages, but in our family, we don't snap at people that way, not at a boss, a teacher, a coworker, another family member—and *never, ever* at our spouse! We do our best to treat each other with respect and consideration at all times because that's what God wants us to do. Well, I had blown it. After just a few seconds I started fretting and talking to God, and then I quickly climbed back in the car and, in tears, let Dawn, my best friend, know that I knew how sinful I had just been. Putting herself last, as always, she forgave me with the alacrity of one who has been deeply forgiven herself. Then I got back out, pulled the gas hose all the way around to the opposite side of the car, and began pumping gas.

Deep Friendships Affect Friends Deeply

When you really love someone, it hurts you when you hurt that person. An intentional or unintentional strike at a loved one boomerangs back to you and rips you apart inside because you are affected by what affects the person you love. The closer your connection with the other person, the more deeply it hurts, whether you are the one who is wounded or the one who does the wounding. This should not surprise us, because intimate friendships naturally invite a deeper level of vulnerability. In fact, such reactions serve as a signal or checkpoint of whether a relationship is robust and healthy.

I believe the same holds true for our relationship with Jesus. When you sin, are you torn up or unsettled until you get things ironed out with God? Are you sad that you have hurt the One you love? If so, that reaction is a sign of a healthy relationship with Christ. It reflects a growing level of intimacy with God. It shows that you've become last and he's become first. It says that you care about what he thinks, what is pleasing to him, and what will bring joy to his heart.

On the other hand, if you've just been breezing along on the highway of life, rolling with the punches, and doing the best you can, then you may need to spend time alone with God and honestly evaluate your relationship with him. Are you close enough to him to even care what he thinks? If not, that breaks God's heart. And if you never experience the good kind of guilt as a result of your sin, that's a sure sign that you're putting yourself first rather than last.

A healthy relationship with Christ will be a heartfelt one. It will affect you deeply. You will care about whether or not you are pleasing him. You'll know when you've failed or disappointed him the way the people in Nazareth did. You'll have a sense of joy when you are living a life of faith, like the Roman officer's.

God offers each of us the adventurous privilege of being his friend: "You are my friends if you do what I command" (John 15:14). How connected are you to Jesus? Has your life brought him gladness lately, or has it broken his heart? Is he "amazed" at your faith and godly actions, or is he dumbfounded and hurt by the lack of them? Do you care? He does. He wants you to become last so that he can be first.

10

Learning to Love in the Trenches

"Being Last" by Living Your Life in the Trenches

Some of the most touching and powerful biblical accounts are those that show God's children boldly taking on challenges, acting in blind faith, reaching out to lepers, loving the lonely, feeding the hungry, and healing the sick and brokenhearted. Certainly such acts require that we put our own interests on the back burner and choose to be last, but they also require something else: They require that we get into the trenches, reach out to strangers, and do what other people are unwilling to do. We need to take some risks and rely on God to meet our needs.

One cold, snowy Christmas Day in Washington, D.C., I went downtown with my friends Mark and James to hand out sandwiches to the poor. I recall that day vividly, especially because of a young African-American man we met, whose hands were discolored from the freezing temperatures. When I told him we had come to share some good food as well as Jesus' love, he grabbed my hand with both of his and held on tight. His hands were like ice, but I don't think it was just the frigid temperatures that made him cling to me. I think he was desperate for human contact. The night before, he had been attacked by hoodlums, who hit him with bricks and stole the bag containing all of his possessions. That bag was all he had, and they took it.

When we found out his jacket was among the missing items, James ran back to our car and got an extra jacket Mark had brought along. All the while, that man held my hand in his; he just couldn't get enough human touch. That experience has become unforgettable. The man's eyes and the firmness of his grip often come back to me. I learned something new about love that snowy Christmas afternoon: Real love breaks through barriers, and consideration for other people gains top priority. Real love is being last. My hope is to practice that kind of love each day, no matter whom God puts in my path.

Family Problems

Let's take a minute to consider an important question: Why should someone who is not a Christian want to be in the family of God? What's so attractive about Christianity?

In chapter 7 we talked about how different from "the world" the family of God is supposed to be. We are to live like aliens or foreigners because this world is not our home. But what happens when the same divisions, fighting, name-calling, and gossip that occur within non-Christian families, businesses, and organizations occur within the church? This is not the way Jesus intended for us to live. In fact, at the Last Supper he outlined a plan that was drastically different:

> I am giving you a new commandment: Love each other. Just as I have loved you, you should love each other. Your love for one another will prove to the world that you are my disciples.
> JOHN 13:34-35

If these verses tell us how the family of God was designed to function, then we have some family problems. The backbiting and power struggles going on in many of our churches send a negative message. And it's not happening just in churches. Christians out in society are guilty of these things as well. We need to change the message we're sending—and we can.

But change needs to begin with me personally and with you personally. I truly believe that by choosing to be last, we can restore love and compassion within the family of God, one person at a time, and take it to a hurting world. The apostle Paul gives us some great advice on one of the ways we can be last:

Whenever we have the opportunity, we should do good to everyone—especially to those in the family of faith.
GALATIANS 6:10

Whenever you have a chance to encourage another Christian, or anyone else, take advantage of the opportunity. Do you remember what Jesus identified as the second-greatest commandment?

Love your neighbor as yourself. MATTHEW 22:39

Here's some deceptively simple but powerful advice: Don't think about yourself so much. Jesus has provided everything his followers need. He knows what we need before we ask, and it gives him joy when we trust him to meet our needs and then spend our time and energy reaching out to others and sharing his love with them.

But Jesus knows that barriers exist in the human heart, and in one biblical event he exposes those barriers and shows us the right way to love one another.

Three Times, Three Questions

When a story appears in the Bible, we can be sure that it's important. But when the same story appears repeatedly, then from God's perspective, it's critical. Indeed, I think it's a lesson about love that's staring us right in the face. That's the case in the account of the leper, which occurs in three different books of the Bible.

To help you see what Jesus is saying in this story, I want you to think about three questions:

1. Am I judgmental?
2. Am I exclusive?
3. Am I approachable?

Now, while you ponder those questions, let's look at what happened when Jesus met the leper:

> Large crowds followed Jesus as he came down the mountainside. Suddenly, a man with leprosy approached him and knelt before him. "Lord," the man said, "if you are willing, you can heal me and make me clean."
>
> Jesus reached out and touched him. "I am willing," he said. "Be healed!" And instantly the leprosy disappeared.
> MATTHEW 8:1-3

Do you realize how culturally unacceptable it was for this leper to run up to Jesus and speak to him? The very presence of lepers was considered abhorrent, and the lives of those infected were characterized by isolation and shame. People with leprosy had to live out their lives in specially designated areas known as leper colonies. They understood only too well the pain of isolation. We don't know the exact details of this man's leprosy, but one passage defines his case as severe. He may have been a leper since childhood. He may have been taken away from his family at a young age, or his whole family may have been leprous and were forced to live in the colony. What we do know is something about the horrific effects of this disease.

In the beginning, leprosy slowly turns the skin into an abnormal white or red color, and the hair of some lepers becomes completely white. As the disease progresses, the peripheral nervous system begins to fail, and sufferers lose the ability to feel pain. Lepers might cut themselves and not know it or go about their lives oblivious to the fact that untreated infections are slowly taking over their bodies. Over time, the degeneration of the body's nerves can result in the gradual loss of extremities—fingers, ears, toes—or at least in extreme swelling. Eyebrows and eyelashes come off, and scabs form from head to toe. Voice boxes and throats can degenerate to the point where speaking and eating become difficult, if not impossible.

Am I Judgmental?

Because healthy people were afraid of contracting the disease, lepers were required to shout, "Unclean! Unclean!" as they walked in public so that people standing nearby could stay at least six feet away from them. Imagine how it hurt those who were infected. No one wanted to associate with them.

The odor of leprosy's severe tissue degeneration caused the religious leaders in some Jewish traditions to observe a policy of "downwind distance." If the religious leaders were standing downwind from a leper, the leper had to be at least fifty yards (150 feet!) away. Imagine the message this conveyed, when the official representatives of God considered lepers detestable, even sinful. Are *we* judgmental?

The convicting reality is, Christ's followers struggled with loving others back then, and two thousand years later, many of us still do.

Am I Exclusive?

With all the obvious effects of leprosy and all the rules surrounding it, how did the leper in Matthew 8 even manage to get close to Jesus? I don't know the answer to that question, but I do know that the first thing the leper did when he got to Jesus was hit the ground. He didn't even say anything first, he just bowed down! There are times when we should approach Jesus like that—just keep our mouths shut and bow down to him. That's a true sign of being last. At any rate, this leprous man knew that Jesus deserved to be honored and worshiped, that he had power over disease, and that he was different from any other man in the crowd. So convinced was he of these facts that it was only *after* he had bowed that he said, "Lord, if you are willing, you can heal me and make me clean."

If Jesus had followed the usual policies concerning lepers, he would have shot back six feet and told the sick man to hit the road. Instead, he stood right where he was and refused to back away, as everyone else in the leper's life would have done. He refused to exclude the leper from what he offered to others. We saw in the preceding paragraph that the leper acted (bowed) before he spoke. Jesus decided to return the favor, and in doing so, he made an extraordinary statement before speaking even a word. He did what no other person would have done: He "reached out and touched him"! He put his clean hands on the unclean. And only *after* Jesus had touched him did he speak. Jesus included this man with all the other recipients of his love and care. He lived out his compassion in a very real action of love—an action that I'm positive the leprous man and the onlookers would never forget.

Am I Approachable?

One of Christ's most amazing qualities was—and still is—his approachability. Jesus welcomed the leper the same way he did other people, because to Jesus, they were all the same! It didn't matter to him whether you were sick, repulsive, or demon controlled. It didn't matter what kind of job you had or what kind of life you had lived before. Jesus let anyone come to him, and he reached out with compassion. He put others first, and we need to learn to follow his lead.

A Touch of Love

Many of us—whether we realize it or not—keep ourselves isolated from situations in which it is difficult to love. That's why when I speak at Christian colleges or high schools, I encourage people to put themselves into just those kinds of situations. For instance, if a boy tells me about his desire to do a meaningful service project, I suggest a difficult one.

First, I might ask him where the nearest hospital is that houses AIDS or cancer patients. Then, I encourage him to have a school official coordinate a time with the hospital when he and some other students can visit the patients. The objective is to give those patients a touch of love. Speak with them. Pray for them. And most of all, to physically touch those people whose only contact of late has been with medical devices and latex gloves. Just hold their hands while you talk. Listen to their stories. Look them in the eye, and love them. Put them first and yourself last. This is what Jesus would do.

Love Power

Jesus never rejects those who come to him humbly and respectfully. In fact, he doesn't stop with just *touching* the leper; he says he wants to *heal* him. Jesus' heart fills with compassion, he reaches out in love, and he gives a precise command, "Be healed!" and instantly—instantly—the leprosy disappears. Can you imagine the man's bright white hair flashing back to its original color and the discoloration of his skin regaining its natural pigment? Did his voice slowly return to normal as he thanked Jesus? I wish I could have been there!

Reviewing a Lesson in Love

By the time Jesus finished healing the man with leprosy, he had shown his disciples how to love. First, he was not *judgmental*. In other words, the man's leprosy did not become a sickening roadblock that stopped Jesus from entering his world. Second, Jesus was not *exclusive* or too proud to be associated with a leper. If you want to love someone, you need to stop caring so much about protecting yourself and start interacting with the people with whom you may have been too proud to interact in the past. Third, he was *approachable*. He didn't shy away from someone whom society considered disgusting.

My Friend Frank

I wasn't always the best Christian role model back in high school. In fact, for the most part, my interests were wrapped up in sports and girls. Because of that, I missed a number of opportunities to love people. But there is one opportunity that I did not miss, and for that I am grateful to God and pleased with how he chose to act in and through my life.

Each day at lunch, Frank (not his real name) sat by himself. I don't mean he sat with a few other guys who didn't fit in. I mean Frank was alone. He had a difficult time speaking clearly, was unable to walk like everyone else, and had some other obvious deficiencies. Because of those strikes against him, Frank was labeled socially inadequate, became the butt of many thoughtless jokes, and was avoided by others, much like the leper in Matthew 8.

I must admit that for a long time, I treated Frank the same way everyone else did. I had earned my reputation by scoring more than a thousand points in my varsity basketball career, so naturally, at lunch you'd find me sitting with the jocks and cheerleaders; I thought I had all the friends I needed.

One day, however, my friend Ehrin and I got sick of seeing Frank alone, so we decided to sit with him during lunch. As we walked to his table, I felt as if every eye in the cafeteria was on us. I could imagine a hundred people thinking, *They're not supposed to be sitting there. They're part of the popular crowd.* I felt as if I was breaking some unspoken rule, but that rule needed to be broken.

In no time some of the other guys hesitantly asked if they could join us, and soon we were introducing everyone to our new friend, Frank. Even the girls came over to sit with us. Before long, it seemed as if half the school wanted to hang out at Frank's table. Eventually, Ehrin and I couldn't even find a seat! Of course, there were some people who still didn't get it. But all it took for some change was one time, just being last *one time*. We decided to reach out to Frank, and his whole high school experience was changed for the better.

As I reflect on that time now, I think Frank was a Christian. That made him my brother. So when none of us Christians sat with him at lunch, his own family was rejecting him. Think about how it would feel to be disowned by your mom or dad, your brothers or sisters. That is what Frank had felt every day. He felt the brunt of God's family problems—until a few of us became last, took a risk, stepped out of our comfort zones, and reached out to a heart in need. Frank, if you're reading this, I'm sorry it took us so long to get to your table.

Just Kidding!

How often do you hear those words? I'm willing to bet that if someone makes a negative comment, often those are the next words you hear. In our society, conversations are frequently peppered with put-downs. People break others down so that they can be first and feel better about themselves. The family of God should be different, but often it seems that the only difference is that we tend to tack "just kidding" on to belittling comments we make, as if those words somehow take the sting out of what we've said and make the verbal jabs acceptable or inoffensive.

Whether or not you think making sarcastic "jokes" about someone else's character is a sin or not, the fact is that such jokes do not encourage others or build them up. On the contrary, they trouble and tear down. It's not difficult to figure out which is better: a compliment or a bad joke. Sincere compliments can lift people's spirits just when they need it most. You can't say the same about all sarcasm, so whether you realize it or not, many sarcastic jokes about other people are sin. The Scriptures remind us how important it is to think before we speak and to choose our words carefully: "Let everything you say be good and helpful, so that your words will be an encouragement to those who hear them" (Ephesians 4:29). Therefore, we could say that anything we say that is unhelpful is discouraging and sinful. Our words are supposed to encourage those who hear them. The book of James warns, "Remember, it is sin to know what you ought to do and then not do it" (4:17).

Are you an encourager or a discourager? Do you make an effort to see and point out the God-given brilliance in the actions and attitudes of others, or are you part of a clique whose "members" look down on people who aren't like them? Jesus wants our lives to be marked by an overflow of love for everyone around us. He wants us to use our words to build others up, not to tear them down. Can you remember the last time you made a conscious choice to compliment someone as you entered a room?

Love goes far beyond mere words, though. Verbal compliments are great, but we need to solidify our words by following them up with active love and service. Real love looks on people with compassion and then reaches out to them. Can you remember the last time you encouraged someone with your words *and* your actions? Love expresses itself in a combination of words and deeds. Jesus did, and he asks us to do the same.

Reaching Out—In Review

How did you do on those questions I asked you to think about? Let's look at them once again:

+ *Are you judgmental?* Do you label people by what they look like, how they talk or act, how much money they make, who their families are, or where they live?

+ *Are you exclusive?* Do you already have an "inner circle" of friends? Do you spend time only with certain people, go only to certain places, and never take time or the opportunity to step outside your comfort zone?
+ *Are you approachable?* Do you find yourself looking down on certain people and not wanting to be associated with them—even other Christians because of the differences between you?

If the crowds on the mountainside in Matthew 8 had been honest, I wonder whether they would have answered yes to the first two questions and no to the third one. I can imagine them yelling at the leper as he came toward Jesus: "Get away from him! Back your unclean, leprous self six feet away, or you're going to get pelted with rocks!" Would they have acted as if they were better than the leper or were somehow "responsible" for the fact that they were healthy, while his uncleanness was clearly the result of some sin he had committed?

If we don't want those attitudes to characterize us, we need to pay close attention to these words:

If anyone claims, "I am living in the light," but hates a Christian brother or sister, that person is still living in darkness.
1 JOHN 2:9

If someone says, "I love God," but hates a Christian brother or sister, that person is a liar; for if we don't love people we can see, how can we love God, whom we cannot see?
1 JOHN 4:20

Jesus teaches us to be last, to love others, and to put their needs before our own. He says that it's no great feat to love those who love us; the real trick lies in being able to genuinely love the "unlovely." Throughout the Bible, we see lessons in how the family of God should relate. But once again, that requires us to be last and to let our judgmental, exclusive attitudes and our lack of approachability fall by the wayside.

It's time for us to sacrifice our own pride, learn to be last, and really love those who are different from us. Jesus sacrificed his life for us while we were sinners. It's time we passed along the same compassion that changed our eternal destiny.

> If we love our Christian brothers and sisters, it proves that we have passed from death to life. But a person who has no love is still dead. . . . Dear children, let's not merely say that we love each other; let us show the truth by our actions.
>
> 1 JOHN 3:14, 18

Conclusion

Do you remember the graduation story I told at the beginning of the book? On the day that we "graduate" from this life, we will stand "on a stage" before God. First Corinthians 3 says that all we've done on earth will be judged. It could be a really great experience. The question is, will Jesus think we did a great job of living our life on earth?

Jesus said, "So you want first place? Then take the last place" (Mark 9:35, *The Message*). As we've seen, true greatness comes from making a conscious choice to be last in *every* area of our lives:

What does that look like in practical terms? Jesus showed us at every turn:

> + *Live a life of service:* "[Jesus] got up from the table, took off his robe, wrapped a towel around his waist, and poured water into a basin. Then he began to wash the disciples' feet, drying them with the towel he had around him" (John 13:4-5).
> + *Life a life of mercy:* "'Which of these three would you say was a neighbor to the man who was attacked by

bandits?' Jesus asked. The man replied, 'The one who showed him mercy.' Then Jesus said, 'Yes, now go and do the same'" (Luke 10:33-37).

+ *Live a life of sacrifice:* "Give your bodies to God because of all he has done for you. Let them be a living and holy sacrifice—the kind he will find acceptable. This is truly the way to worship him" (Romans 12:1).

+ *Live a life of love:* "Let love be your highest goal!" (1 Corinthians 14:1).

+ *Live a life of humility:* "Though [Jesus] was God, he did not think of equality with God as something to cling to. Instead, he gave up his divine privileges; he took the humble position of a slave and was born as a human being" (Philippians 2:6-7).

+ *Live a life of submission:* "[Jesus] went on a little farther and bowed with his face to the ground, praying, 'My Father! If it is possible, let this cup of suffering be taken away from me. Yet I want your will to be done, not mine'" (Matthew 26:39).

+ *Live life as an alien:* [Peter said,] "I warn you as 'temporary residents and foreigners' to keep away from worldly desires that wage war against your very souls. Be careful to live properly among your unbelieving neighbors. Then even if they accuse you of doing wrong, they will see your honorable behavior, and they will give honor to God when he judges the world" (1 Peter 2:11-12).

+ *Live a life of confession:* [David said,] "I confessed all my sins to you and stopped trying to hide my guilt.

I said to myself, 'I will confess my rebellion to the Lord.' And you forgave me! All my guilt is gone" (Psalm 32:5).

+ *Live a life that causes positive amazement:* "Whenever we have the opportunity, we should do good to everyone—especially to those in the family of faith" (Galatians 6:10).

+ *Live your life in the trenches:* "A man with leprosy approached [Jesus] and knelt before him. 'Lord,' the man said, 'if you are willing, you can heal me and make me clean.' Jesus reached out and touched him. 'I am willing,' he said. 'Be healed!'" (Matthew 8:2-3).

Being last isn't easy. It can be messy. It caused Jesus to get "down and dirty" to wash the disciples' feet. It caused him to touch and spend time with those whom society shunned. Indeed, it cost Jesus everything he had to give. But if our desire is to follow him and be truly "great" in his Kingdom, he will take delight in helping us to live as he did, and our lives will bring him great joy.

A Note on Understanding the Bible

As curious and independent human beings, we often want to know more about everything (while pretending that we already do). However, our desire to know is often guided only by our latest whims. By nature, we do not really want our search for knowledge to be directed by someone or something else. So when we come to the Bible, we expect to ask our own questions and get our own answers.

Unfortunately, it doesn't work that way with the Bible. We do not get to tell God what he should talk about in the Bible and then go find where he has hidden what we want to know. Instead, we are forced to face the fact that the Bible has limited information and therefore does not always answer our questions. So we must decide: Do we want to listen to what God has chosen to say, or do we want to manipulate the text so that it relates to our own questions? This is an important decision and one readers have often bypassed or overlooked. When *we* try to call the shots instead of relying on the original Author to determine how we read and understand the Bible, we end up with an excess of Christian "answers" to questions that the Bible doesn't even address.

Here are a few examples: Maybe you want to know what Jesus was like as a teenager but the Bible does not really talk about that subject. You wonder whether Jesus was a good singer, but the Bible tells you only that he sang psalms after Passover like everyone else. It doesn't mention anything about whether he sang on key. You might want to know if he had above-average physical abilities and could run fast or jump high. But your quest for an answer is doomed from the start, because the Bible shows no interest in those questions. So you change your approach to a more theological question, such as whether Jesus knew as an infant that he was the Messiah. Your desire to know these things is normal and healthy for a human being, but your search for answers will turn out to be pointless if the questions you ask don't reflect the concerns of the original writers of the books in the Bible. When that's the case, what you're really doing is spending time in an imaginative exercise to *create answers* rather than in a critical effort to learn the truth.

The fact that you have a question does not guarantee that the Bible will answer it (although if your question is valid, the Bible more often than not will help you out). So how can you carefully and humbly study the Bible so that your investigation is directed by God's agenda rather than by your own personal or theological interests? The answer to that question lies in one word: *context*.

Context Is King

What is context? The *American Heritage Dictionary of the English Language* (fourth edition, 2004) defines *context* as "the circumstances in which an event occurs"; in other words, the setting. When you study the Bible, the key to understanding what God wants you to know is to read the passage in light of its context. You can do that by following two guiding principles.

First, pay attention to what the biblical authors emphasize. Take the Gospels, for example. The authors don't seem concerned with Jesus' life as a teenager or for the development of his messianic self-consciousness, but they do emphasize his stories (we call them parables). Matthew, Mark, and Luke portray Jesus as a master storyteller who takes stock of his audience and then delivers stories that communicate powerfully and effectively to the crowd at hand. So if we want to avoid following our personal agendas and instead follow the focus of the Bible, we can start by asking about the points of Jesus' parables.

Second, look for the meaning of a passage in its historical context rather than in your own experience. Instead of searching your past for experiences that tie in with the story that Jesus told, ask questions like these: Who are the characters in the story? How do those characters relate to Jesus' audience? What did Jesus' audience know about the story from common cultural and written traditions that I do not? These questions about the historical context of Jesus' teaching help you to take off your twenty-first-century perspective and view the stories through the eyes of a Jewish commoner who heard Jesus' stories firsthand.

Studying the Bible with these two principles in mind will help you to ask the questions that God considered most important to address and then to recognize his answers. And remember, context is king!

About the Author

Jeremy Kingsley is the founder and president of Onelife Ministries and has been an itinerant communicator since 1996. A highly respected teacher, he is one of the most sought-after speakers today. Jeremy has spoken to hundreds of thousands of people in the United States and has also been involved in ministry in Africa, Mongolia, India, and Central America. He holds degrees from Columbia International University. He and his wife, Dawn, and their sons, Jaden and Dylan, live in South Carolina.

JEREMY KINGSLEY is a Bible teacher and a leader for a new generation. At universities, music festivals, corporate functions, and conferences in the United States and abroad, he has challenged hundreds of thousands:

"Don't read the Bible to finish, read it to change"
and *"The path to true greatness lies in humility and service."*

Jeremy is passionate about knowing Christ and making him known. A talented and creative communicator, he has become one of the most sought-after speakers in the country.

Would you like
to have Jeremy Kingsley, author of
Be Last: Descending to Greatness,
speak at your event?

Contact:
ONELIFE MINISTRIES
143 Killian Point Circle
Chapin, SC 29036

(803) 315-2788

Learn more about Jeremy Kingsley and Onelife Ministries
on the Web: www.jeremykingsley.com.

CP0247